Infidelity

Tools and Exercises to Rebuild Your Relationship

(How to Catch a Cheating Spouse in Infidelity Having an Emotional)

Lewis Pennington

Published By **Andrew Zen**

Lewis Pennington

Infidelity: Tools and Exercises to Rebuild Your Relationship (How to Catch a Cheating Spouse in Infidelity Having an Emotional)

ISBN 978-1-988842-05-9

No part of this guidebook shall be reproduced in any form without permission in writing from the publisher except in the case of brief quotations embodied in critical articles or reviews.

Legal & Disclaimer

The information contained in this book is not designed to replace or take the place of any form of medicine or professional medical advice. The information in this book has been provided for educational & entertainment purposes only.

The information contained in this book has been compiled from sources deemed reliable, and it is accurate to the best of the Author's knowledge; however, the Author cannot guarantee its accuracy and validity and cannot be held liable for any errors or omissions. Changes are periodically made to this book. You must consult your doctor or get professional medical advice before using any of the suggested remedies, techniques, or information in this book.

Upon using the information contained in this book, you agree to hold harmless the Author from and against any damages, costs, and expenses, including any legal fees potentially resulting from the application of any of the information provided by this guide. This disclaimer applies to any damages or injury caused by the use and application, whether directly or indirectly, of any advice or information presented, whether for breach of contract, tort, negligence, personal injury, criminal intent, or under any other cause of action.

You agree to accept all risks of using the information presented inside this book. You need to consult a professional medical practitioner in order to ensure you are both able and healthy enough to participate in this program.

Table Of Contents

Chapter 1: Understanding Betrayal

As a counselor, I've heard many tragic and tough testimonies through the years. I remember one customer coming to me no longer lengthy after she'd damaged up collectively alongside her boyfriend. She suggested me that she'd skipped paintings so she must put together a wonder celebration for her ex. She'd lengthy past out of her manner to ask all his buddies, going via his social media to ensure that everybody he knew is probably there.

Unfortunately, she had no idea that one of the human beings she invited became an ex-woman buddy. An ex-girl friend it have become out he though had feelings for. The pair of them ended up hooking up at the birthday celebration, no longer being involved who noticed them.

To make topics worse, on the identical time as my client once more to artwork, she had been given fired for her unauthorized absence.

There became each different patron who had surely located out her husband have become dishonest. She'd in recent times given beginning to their first infant and had had to take a month off sex to permit her frame get better. Her husband reputedly didn't need to attend a month to have his desires fulfilled, so he downloaded Tinder and went on a number of dates. The quality reason she discovered out end up because of the fact certainly one in every of her buddies got here within the route of his Tinder profile.

The first patron cut up up along with her companion and is now luckily married to someone else. Believe it or no longer, the second one patron managed to work matters thru together together with her husband, and that they've had greater babies—this time without any cheating!

Infidelity can seem to everybody, and it's by no means the fault of the character being cheated on—some issue they will need to say. If you're unhappy in a relationship, there are numerous different things you could do to alternate your state of affairs that don't incorporate slumbering with someone else.

WHAT'S A NORMAL REACTION TO DISCOVERING INFIDELITY?

Being cheated on is one of the maximum painful studies for anyone. It doesn't don't forget if the affair modified into cutting-edge or occurred a long term ago and has handiest simply come to mild. It hurts to understand you've been betrayed.

People often question me, "Is how I'm feeling regular?" The fact is that there are a number of reactions to infidelity, and every unmarried one is 'everyday.' For many, mastering your loved one is dishonest on you triggers a bodily reaction. The annoying device comes online, forcing a powerful response which could move again on every occasion we're confronted with a reminder of the affair, making us experience like we're mastering about it for the primary time all all all over again.

Since the fearful device is worried, you may be in a persistent state of 'fight, flight, or freeze.'

Fight. Many people who've suffered infidelity discover themselves turning into indignant and irritable. After all, they've been betrayed inside the worst viable way. They concept they could receive as real with the concepts in their relationship, and rather, it appears like any shared values are a dim and remote memory. This can bring about an explosive outburst of anger or a normal motion of anger and aggression. Alternatively, they may constantly ask their accomplice questions or call for in-intensity knowledge about them. While this behavior is completely normal, it's now not a

4

wholesome or sustainable manner to be in a relationship. Your anger can be definitely justified; letting that anger spill into physical or emotional abuse isn't. Interrogating your partner isn't always going to construct don't forget. Letting anger rule you for too lengthy will depart you and your partner emotionally exhausted, and it will likely be tough to rebuild your connection.

Flight. Some people leave the immediately they discover about an affair. Again, that is flawlessly ordinary and natural. For a few, this departure is for correct. For others, it's a miles-needed time to way and make feel of their enjoy. However, letting this damage move on for too extended will make it difficult if you need to art work through it collectively. What would possibly have started as a brief pause for breath turns into eternal, regardless of the reality that that wasn't what you wanted.

Freeze. You may additionally experience emotionally numb at the same time as you discover you've been cheated on. This can be less hard than dealing with the pain without delay. This reaction can also additionally moreover take many splendid office work—you'll in all likelihood bury your self in paintings, spend hours playing video video video games, or start making plans for what lifestyles is going to be like without your partner at the same time as although maintaining the relationship within the period in-between. Blocking out the ache could in all likelihood seem like the smooth choice, however until you withstand it, you won't be capable of deal with it and ultimately skip beyond it.

There also are not unusual reactions from the cheater, who may be handling their very very own traumatic conditions:

Defensiveness. Some unfaithful spouses find out themselves trying to defend what they've accomplished, whether or no longer or not it is the affair itself or the behavior surrounding the affair. It can be tough to stand up to the way you've negatively affected someone else, and being predicted to continuously display or deliver an reason behind your self can reason defensiveness or possibly resentment.

Impatience. This might be the most common response I see. Many untrue spouses definitely want to transport on and discover it hard to understand why their accomplice remains hung up at the affair. It is comprehensible that a dishonest associate who has made a preference to recommit to the connection have to need to move on short, but there may be despite the fact that restoration that desires to be finished, and that takes time. In addition, it can be tough to check the motives why a person cheated and what needs to be completed to repair and rebuild.

Grief. This is one of the maximum complicated reactions to an affair and in all likelihood the hardest for the betrayed associate to come back returned again to phrases with. Affairs usually arise for a motive which can be due to a want that modified into no longer met within the courting. So, a person can be grieving the dearth of a relationship even while being committed to creating their marriage artwork. It is vital to in fact take delivery of this grief and permit time to way it.

SHAME

A not unusual reaction for every occasions is shame. Shame approximately having an affair and shame approximately being cheated on. In truth, I've determined that the overwhelming majority of couples pick out out to cowl the fact of the affair, whether or not or no longer they actively agreed to accomplish that or now not. There seems to be a consensus that infidelity is embarrassing. What's greater, at the same time as you would possibly apprehend the cheater feeling embarrassed approximately what they've done, I've determined that the dedicated partner feels it all the more.

There is a revel in that they must be people who honestly did a few factor wrong. It's their fault the wedding faltered. Of course, it isn't, but because while had been emotions logical?

Another trouble can be that the betrayed accomplice desires to preserve things thriller due to the fact they're afraid that if the reality came out, it'd disenchanted the cheater, who would probably give up the connection actually. Thus, neither partner experience capable of be completely open, and recall becomes more hard and harder to build.

For the person who cheated, it may be hard to just accept that they behaved that manner, especially if their self-picture is taken into consideration one of integrity. They won't have concede to have an affair. It certainly passed off.

Facing as plenty as shame is reasonably vital in overcoming it. Ignoring any emotional feelings doesn't purpose them to depart. In truth, it most effective creates greater troubles. You may additionally discover yourself turning to horrible coping techniques, which encompass ingesting, tablets, overeating, or even excessive exercising. Not quality will those no longer cope with the shame, but they'll also make you experience worse about yourself.

Find someone you can communicate to approximately your disgrace. This may be a relied on pal or a therapist. Talking about your emotions with out feeling judged will assist you accept, system, and flow past them.

WHAT IS INFIDELITY ANYWAY?

Infidelity also may be referred to as cheating or adultery. It is the act of being worried in emotional or sexual intimacy with a person outside of the agreed boundaries of your relationship. It does no longer must comprise sexual interest and may take place in person or on line.

It may be hard to make sure your companion is devious on you while not having direct proof. However, there are commonly a few crimson flags so that you can offer you with a sign of what's taking area. These may additionally encompass:

Your associate is lots much less inquisitive about intercourse.

Your companion may also want you to be worried in sexual acts that you find out foreign or off-placing.

Your companion takes greater care over their look.

Your partner can be having issues dozing.

Your associate can also moreover seem distracted or burdened.

Your partner can also call for extra privateness than stylish.

Your accomplice can also want to spend more time on my own or be away from home more regularly.

Your accomplice may be more negative or competitive than traditional.

You may also additionally moreover locate your self tormented by insomnia, pressure, or distraction due to the fact you're suspicious of your partner.

Believe it or now not, there are eleven one-of-a-kind sorts of infidelity:

1.   Conflict avoidance affairs. When a accomplice actively seeks to avoid any form of battle, they may have an affair to meet their desires which can't be expressed to their spouse. These affairs generally don't final lengthy but can also recur normally.

2.   Intimacy avoidance affairs. When someone is scared of intimacy, they'll use an affair to keep an emotional distance among themselves and their partner. As with war

avoidance affairs, they'll be inclined now not to very last extended however regularly are repeated. However, if both partners are intimacy avoiders, affairs like the ones also can help them maintain an emotionally a ways off courting.

three. Individual/existential/developmental-based totally honestly affairs. Midlife crises, empty nest syndrome, melancholy, or a modern-day experience of vacancy can all be triggers for an affair. The affected partner may additionally additionally take a lover to rediscover themselves or cope with anxiety, despair, or one in all a kind horrible feelings bobbing up from the strain of coping with the growing antique way or a loss of non secular fulfillment. An affair can be their way of feeling attractive all over again or seeking to meet superb goals or fantasies instead of any dissatisfaction with the wedding itself.

4.   Sexual addiction affairs. Sex addicts have horrible impulse control, the usage of

sex to masks their inner ache and angst. They are drawn to the fun of an orgasm but then have to cope with the come down into shame and worthlessness.

5.   Accidental-quick affairs. This is the kind of affair that 'certainly occurs' because of the reality a person is inside the wrong place on the right time. It is unplanned and may stand up due to interest, pity, drunkenness, and so forth., ensuing in a brief and typically one-off affair.

6.   Philandering. Some human beings are more likely to cheat, whether or now not because of loss of self guarantee, low arrogance, or a need for outside validation. Narcissistic and impulsive humans are specially probable to have interaction in this shape of affair. Philanderers view extramarital sex as a few difficulty they're entitled to and might be satisfied to take advantage of any opportunities supplying themselves without feeling any guilt about it.

7.   Retribution affairs. These upward push up due to the reality one associate looks like they want to get revenge on the opportunity. There can be many reasons for this—it might be the opportunity companion cheated, or has withheld coins, love, or emotion, or they will have performed a few factor else the companion felt emerge as an injustice.

eight. Bad marriage affairs. These come approximately because of the fact a wedding suffers from terrible communication or a lack of intimacy and/or guide. There also can be factors regarding incompatible cultural and familial values. When a marriage is unhappy, one or every partners can also look for a solution in an extramarital affair.

nine. Exit affairs. These are used as an excuse to cease a marriage, whether or not or not deliberate or not. They regularly bring about a partner having a modern relationship in place earlier than leaving the wedding, just so they don't must be by myself.

10.   Parallel lives affairs. These are lengthy-term affairs with a second accomplice. The high-quality associate can be privy to such an affair and tolerate it without ever right now addressing it.

11.   Online affairs. These have turn out to be increasingly more common due to the accessible, an awful lot much less high-priced, and nameless nature of the internet. They can also moreover moreover comprise searching a person on-line through video, speakme on instantaneous messenger services, in chatrooms, or thru electronic mail or phone. They can upward thrust up at any time of the day or night time time or perhaps within the own family home at the same time as the other associate is round. The loss of bodily touch all through a sex act can frequently make the relationship even more extreme.

THE IMPACT OF INFIDELITY

The pain due to infidelity may be overwhelming. You may additionally enjoy grief for the relationship you belief you had, anger for being betrayed, or sadness for the lack of all of your hopes and dreams. The effect can be so devastating that Dr. Dennis Ortman defined it as a shape of trauma, calling it 'Post-Infidelity Stress Disorder,'[1] claiming that the stages of recuperation from the trauma of infidelity are akin to the five levels of grief. Research moreover indicates that infidelity can bring about accelerated degrees of tension, depression, and pressure.[2]

However, you're feeling is genuinely valid. Let your enjoy be your experience.

THE LONG-TERM IMPACT OF BEING CHEATED ON

It can take a long time to recover from an affair. When we are in love, the emotion triggers the discharge of oxytocin and dopamine, hormones chargeable for making us sense appropriate. This may be addictive to the mind, so whilst you revel in rejected because of the reality your companion had an affair, it is able to purpose adjustments inside the shape of the thoughts, which may be just like the impact of improving from substance abuse.3 You may also experience comparable signs to PTSD, which incorporates flashbacks, nightmares, and obsessing over what passed off. You may additionally moreover turn out to be overly reactive to any perceived threats, each to yourself or your relationship, and your dozing and ingesting styles may be disturbed.

If you have got got youngsters, they may moreover be affected within the occasion that they discover one in all their dad and mom cheated. They also can decide to detail with the wronged partner, trusting them greater. They also can feel similar emotions to the betrayed partner, in conjunction with confusion, anxiety, abandonment, and isolation. They may war to recollect their personal destiny romantic companions and characteristic horrible ideas round constancy.

There is ideal information, however. It is feasible to heal and circulate on from an affair. Our brains have an capability to have a look at new skills, called neuroplasticity.

One check tested how the brain responds and adapts to honest social encounters versus untrustworthy ones.Four This teaches us who we're able to and can't keep in mind.

Using MRI scans, researchers located that once we experience surprising cooperation from some other man or woman, we change our behavior extra than while we're unexpectedly betrayed. The more social encounters we've, the less our mind responds to untrustworthy human beings.

So the more we deal with untrustworthy humans, the a great deal a good deal less surprised we are with the useful resource of it, but the masses much less we react to it. Conversely, the extra we surround ourselves with sincere humans, the extra we admire it and engage in pro-social behavior. We clearly generally tend to cognizance on those we're able to consider, that lets in you to defend us from being betrayed.

This way that our thoughts adjusts with every revel in so that we are able to pass closer to surrounding ourselves with increasingly more sincere people so we aren't betrayed all over again. This additionally technique that it's herbal to revel in careful of your partner following an affair. It will take time for the ones precise pathways to be rebuilt.

WHY DO PEOPLE CHEAT IN THE FIRST PLACE?

There are many, many precise reasons why someone would likely cheat:

They may be truely predisposed. One form of man or woman check measures how a person ranks for agreeableness, conscientiousness, openness, extraversion and neuroticism, known as the Big Five. When an person rankings low for both agreeableness and conscientiousness, they're more likely to cheat.

Your lives are separated. If you're not sharing significant factors of your lives, one associate may be much more likely to cheat. If you are reserved and distant from your accomplice, it can bring about one in every of you identifying to assemble a lifestyles with a person else.

You war to definitely accept your versions. While opposites can also enchantment to, they may moreover find out it difficult to keep a protracted-time period dating. While someone's variations may additionally to begin with be attractive and a manner of balancing you out, over time, the ones variations can pressure a wedge amongst you as a pair.

One of you develops narcissistic inclinations. All people alternate as we age, whether or now not that be for correct or lousy. If your partner develops narcissistic traits or starts to search for hobby some place else, e.G., flirting with the server even as you go out for a meal collectively, this will be a pink flag for infidelity.

Three vital lessons detail why a person cheats: person, dating, and situational. Individual motives advocate a person has person developments that purpose them to extra inclined to cheat. Religion, politics, and gender might also moreover have a electricity. Relationship reasons suggest someone is feeling sad in their relationship for some thing reason. Situational reasons are the ones external affects that tempt a person to cheat when they wouldn't usually otherwise, e.G., starting a contemporary procedure or moving home.

Within those lessons are a number of specific greater specific reasons:

You've fallen out of love. Many cheaters say they strayed because of the truth both they didn't enjoy like they loved their associate, or that they had more potent feelings for a person else.

You revel in like a trade. Sometimes, human beings experience bored in their courting, so they search for techniques to spice topics up. Or, they might be glad with their companion, however they want to discover splendid factors of themselves. It's extra approximately leaving the person they've come to be in preference to the relationship itself.

You enjoy unnoticed. If you're no longer getting the eye you want from your accomplice, you could decide to search for it a few region else. This is a especially common reason among ladies.

You have been in a specific situation. Not all people plans to have an affair. Someone may additionally find themselves in a hard state of affairs, consisting of having lengthy long past eating or being with someone who makes a pass at them and for a few problem reason, they reciprocate. This is greater common among guys.

You sense the want to decorate your conceitedness or ego. While the prolonged-time period impact of an affair can bring about immoderate, horrible results, inside the second, an affair can provide a person a lift to their ego or conceitedness.

You revel in angry collectively together with your accomplice. You might also additionally have had an trouble with a associate or been going through a hard patch and note an affair as a way of punishing them or getting revenge.

You don't feel dedicated for your companion. If you don't experience together with you're committed to being collectively together with your accomplice, you may determine to stray.

You want to satisfy sexual urges. It may be that the whole lot's extremely good on your dating except your intercourse lifestyles. Maybe you're no longer having as a exceptional deal sex as you need, otherwise you want to have interaction mainly sports your companion won't, so you discover someone else who will meet your sexual goals.

Your testosterone degrees are immoderate if you're male. While hormones aren't an excuse for cheating, there can be proof to expose that if a person's testosterone degrees are excessive, he may additionally revel in extra inclined to cheat. Studies have proven that men in devoted relationships revel in decrease ranges of testosterone and enjoy a good deal a good deal less inclined to cheat, whilst men with better stages of testosterone are extra interested in having intercourse with other humans.Five

You're ovulating if you're woman. Women are more likely to cheat while they may be ovulating and much more likely to get pregnant. Biologically, girls are looking for out the men with the awesome genes to father their youngsters. Men in immoderate call for might not be honest or stick round as quickly due to the fact the toddler is born, so a female in a dedicated courting may additionally experience the urge to cheat all through the fertile a part of her cycle to provide her little one better genes. Again, this isn't an excuse to cheat, however it does provide a hint notion into what might be happening within the body to force nice behaviors.

You're a serial cheater. There is a sure quantity of truth to the saying, as quick as a cheater, normally a cheater. One have a look at decided that someone who had cheated in a relationship have become 3 instances much more likely to cheat on their subsequent partner.6

THE IMPORTANCE OF ADDRESSING BETRAYAL TRAUMA

We've already cited the truth that betrayal can motive trauma. If you've decided you need to maintain your marriage (and if you're reading this ebook, you're at least thinking about it), it's important you face up on your revel in of submit-infidelity trauma ailment.

You have to first recognize that the manner you react to the facts that your partner has had an affair is hardwired into you. Human beings are biologically programmed to bond with their fellow people via constructing deep, nurturing attachments, this means that we're greater willing to look after and defend each one-of-a-kind within the path of attacks. If that bond is broken, it's glaringly traumatizing.

Our stressful device is first rate at identifying a risk however not so nicely at identifying what form of hazard. A betrayal is a totally one-of-a-kind risk to the danger of being eaten via using a tiger, however in your anxious tool, it's all in addition threatening. This is why your feelings may additionally feel scattered whilst you find out your partner has been cheating on you, or you cannot realize what you experience—a smooth sign of trauma.

If the impact of trauma is buried in place of addressed, it is able to purpose prolonged-term problems, wherein you could revel in paranoid or overreact to the smallest things. Given time, you can revel in better, however the ones feelings haven't long lengthy long past away; they've genuinely been buried and are equipped to resurface whilst delivered about.

Dealing with the trauma of an affair might be difficult, however within the long term, it's the healthiest thing to do.

WILL YOU EVER RECOVER FROM AN AFFAIR?

The short solution is nice, no matter whether or not or no longer that's collectively together with your marriage intact or now not. But in case you need your marriage to final, I'm case in point that you may flow into beyond it to a brighter future.

Ideally, you want to get manual from a certified therapist to help you thru the ones tough instances. They will offer you with an independent framework in order to find out your emotions and heal.

We're going to dive deeper into realistic techniques of handling betrayal later in this e-book, however for now, right here are some beginning factors a notable manner to endure in thoughts:

Trust your judgment. If you have got any concerns, some factor in any respect, say so. It doesn't count range whether or not you are correct to your assumptions or not. Right now, what subjects more is that your companion is willing to pay attention and respond on your concerns. If they're not, it will increase questions over whether or not they're going if you want to offer you with the emotional guide you want to get via this.

Don't lower the affair. If you're the only who cheated, it may be tempting to play things down in a bid to make your associate sense better. In truth, this frequently makes subjects worse because of the fact disregarding their fears can come across as in case you've were given greater to cowl.

Keep matters on a want-to-understand foundation. While you'll need assist to get via this, this is exquisite sought from a professional or impartial buddy who will keep place with a purpose to decide what you want to do. If you tell honestly every person what's came about after which determine to live together together with your companion, this may do extreme, or perhaps irreparable, damage in your social network. Some of your friends may also furthermore in no way forgive your companion, even in case you do, that can make subjects tough within the destiny. You may additionally even lose friendships over it.

Make a choice. If you're caught up in a choice among your accomplice or your lover, decide whom you're going to stay with and prevent the opposite dating. If not, what on occasion occurs is that the partner will go along with it because of the truth they're worried approximately being on my own or you have were given children together. The problem with that is that it simplest prolongs the harm. You must every observe artwork to your relationship if you're going to live collectively and then devote. It's the best way ahead. And if you do decide to live collectively, you need to obtain that you'll in no manner see your lover again.

Look at the bigger image. While the cheater is usually the most effective guilty for the affair, it's continually a brilliant idea to keep in mind the kingdom of your relationship at this component. What issues do you have had been given that need to be worked on? Did you start to take each different with no consideration or prevent speakme thru your issues? Identifying modern-day troubles doesn't excuse the affair, however it is able to provide you with a common ground to artwork on inside the destiny.

Give it time. It's going to take at least a one year to recover from being betrayed. It requires consistency and frequently doing what you say you'll do and being in which you are saying you'll be. Know that this stage acquired't final all the time, and subjects gets better in case you're each putting in the strive.

Focus on peace and closure. Eventually, you're going to have to drift beyond this. You can't punish the culprit for all time.

Complete honesty is essential. Get as a top notch deal statistics as you need about the affair to get closure. The unknown is horrifying, so discussing what came about and why permits you to get the information you need to tool the situation after which begin afresh. Let pass of these elements of your relationship which weren't walking and deal with this as an possibility to assemble a present day dynamic to your dating. Things can in no way be the identical another time, however that doesn't mean you can't despite the fact that have a sturdy courting collectively.

In this financial disaster, we've explored the difficulty of infidelity in awesome depth, so that you recognize:

The definition of infidelity.

Reactions to infidelity.

The prolonged-time period impact of infidelity.

The motives for infidelity.

What you may do to begin repairing and rebuilding your courting.

While an affair can be devastating, if each of you're willing to do the hard artwork, it is possible to get better or even see the remarkable problem of a hard situation.

In the following bankruptcy, we'll start this gadget by using digging into the electricity of entire honesty.

Chapter 2: Complete Honesty

"I assume I can rebuild my marriage with out ever telling Becky," John stated in one in all our lessons. "I've ended it with Christina, and I'm inclined to do what it takes to make it as an lousy lot as Becky with out her ever information."

"Do you?" I checked out John impassively, awaiting him to growth on it.

"I propose . . . I anticipate . . . I need . . ." he stuttered and fell into silence.

"Any healthful dating needs to be constructed on honesty," I recommended him. "Maybe Becky doesn't suspect you had an affair, however she'll apprehend some thing is wrong. I'm now not going to inform you that you have to inform her proper now, however I assume you have to remember whether or now not you surely can recovery your marriage with out telling her a few issue this big."

As already mentioned inside the advent, more or less 20% of married men and 13% of married girls cheat. According to a survey completed with the aid of way of Health Testing Centers,1 simply below half of of the humans questioned said they'd cheated in a relationship. Of those, 1/2 of said they knowledgeable their accomplice approximately the affair. Almost half of informed their partner internal constant with week of dishonest, while extra or much less a quarter confessed inner a month, with the rest organized six months or longer to come returned decrease returned clean.

WHY DO PEOPLE CHOOSE TO LIE ABOUT AN AFFAIR?

In my lessons, I've heard every motive practicable why a person doesn't want to inform their spouse about an affair. The maximum common encompass:

I've made my peace with God. Why must I inform my spouse? While I understand and respect every body with sturdy spiritual convictions, in the end, you'll nonetheless need to make topics proper together together with your companion. While dishonesty won't be a lethal sin, it's nevertheless no longer exactly conduct any God should condone.

I'd first-rate be telling my accomplice to make myself revel in better. Really? Confessing to an affair is going to be an emotionally fraught communique for each of you. It's no longer going to make each of you sense pinnacle in the short time period. However, you want to recollect whether or not or no longer you may truly stay with the guilt of what you've completed. Can you have a take a look at your associate without considering the truth they're blissfully unaware you cheated? In the long term, that guilt will do extra damage than specific. While it's going to be frightening in your partner to find out what's took place, normal, it's going to harm you both a whole lot much less than retaining it thriller.

What they don't recognize can't harm them. It's great to assume that is the case, however the truth is that secrets will be inclined to impact our behavior, whether or not we're aware of it or not. Your partner will suspect that something's incorrect, and feeling like you are keeping something from them most absolutely will harm.

They'll leave me. Yes, that's clearly possible. That's the chance you took whilst you made a decision to have an affair. But if you're crucial about making your marriage art work, you'll need to begin with a easy slate and construct on robust foundations. That technique telling them the whole thing and accepting that it can be the end of your dating—or it may be the start of a stronger one.

My associate in reality doesn't suspect a factor. We must definitely keep as we are, couldn't we? Sure, you can. But that's no longer going to recuperation the problems which brought about you having an affair, which means that that there's a hazard you can do it yet again. A courting wants to have complete honesty if it's going to be healthy and thrive. You want to speak about what took place and why.

They received't be able to deal with the truth. Maybe. Again, that's the hazard you took while you cheated. But probably they'll marvel you. You have no idea what their reaction may be until you communicate to them about it.

It come to be most effective a fling. It'll in no way take vicinity over again. Unfortunately, I've determined that the individuals who inform themselves which may be the ones who turn out to be cheating time and again. You need to deal with the basis motives that made you stray, and that's exceptional going to take place in case you communicate it via together together with your companion.

I just want to faux it in no manner came about. I pay hobby that. It's comprehensible to need to behave as though your mistakes didn't seem. But they did. Sticking your head in the sand isn't going to let you treatment the problems to your marriage and gained't assist you in constructing a more potent relationship.

My partner will by no means find out. Maybe no longer. But perhaps they'll. You honestly can't recognize for high-quality. And in case your companion unearths out from a few different deliver, the pain may be that a good buy worse. Thinking you can escape with it's miles going to make you enjoy that you could cheat once more, because of this you'll simplest repeat your mistakes.

THE IMPACT OF DISHONESTY

For many people, on the same time as an affair changed into hurtful, the lies were the most unfavourable aspect. When we find out we've been deceived, it shatters our don't forget in others further to ourselves. We can not rely on our perceptions and evaluations. We revel in like we don't recognize our accomplice the least bit. There's a whole awesome detail to them we did no longer understand about.

Compromise is an crucial a part of a dating. The trouble is that hundreds humans compromise ourselves if you need to make someone else glad. We input into new relationships careworn with the luggage of our past, making it difficult to stop horrible conduct and patterns of conduct we evolved to address past situations. This then impacts how we have interaction with our partners. Maybe we turn out to be jealous or possessive because of the reality we've been cheated on within the beyond, but this then makes us try to manipulate our partner, who then becomes much more likely to have an affair, now not less. Or we don't talk up about topics which might be frightening us, so the trouble gets large and big. Both of you faux the whole lot's desirable sufficient, but one or each of you may start to resent the other, and the relationship will begin to collapse.

When we act with integrity and are sincere about ourselves, we don't need to compromise or act out of any feel of guilt or responsibility. What's greater, we aren't inadvertently pushing our companion to compromise themselves either. The greater open and sincere a pair is with each other, the more wholesome and extra resilient the relationship is. Conversely, the greater lies, deceptions, and secrets and techniques and strategies are normalized, the more likely we are able to get comfortable with huge and big lies.

When you have got were given an affair, mendacity approximately it can help keep the illusion that everything's okay while it isn't. Your associate deserves to recognize that something's incorrect, so that they have got a danger to place it proper. They want to apprehend they may be capable of receive as actual with what you tell them. If lies input into the equation, it's excellent a rely wide variety huge kind of time in advance than the whole lot falls apart.

BEING HONEST AFTER AN AFFAIR

It might sense love it's now not possible to begin another time from a place of honesty while you've lied and cheated or been lied to and cheated on, however it isn't. It will take artwork and time, however it's far viable to get decrease again into a place of don't forget. The most effective relationships are built on a foundation of honesty and transparency. Imagine being capable of be together with your companion, understanding that they love and take delivery of you, irrespective of all of your flaws and faults. What greater proof of love might also moreover want to there be?

When you tell your partner you've had an affair, it can be difficult to understand how hundreds detail to go into. You may additionally need to gloss over what occurred or not want to speak approximately it because you're looking for to located it in the beyond.

If you're the best who've been cheated on, it's a one-of-a-kind story. While your companion has glaringly mentioned about their affair, it's facts to you, so you'll have severa questions. It's very everyday a good way to have pretty a few questions and want to apprehend each little element..

This is the time to be simply honest—cards at the table time. Unless there can be a risk of bodily abuse or suicide, answer any and all questions without prevarication. Trust can handiest be rebuilt if you're sincere from this second beforehand.

This can be more difficult for a few than others. Many humans are used to hiding our feelings, believing that being willing is a weak point and we don't want to be exposed. This can also come from an area of feeling that if our partner is privy to our weaknesses, not simplest will they in no manner accept as true with us once more, however moreover they acquired't love us.

The paradox right right here is that if you could't be honest, you may't be loved for who you are. It's time to try a current way to get the loving, trusting courting you need and deserve.

You'll need to expose you are worth of believe. This may want to likely contain doing some hard matters, collectively with giving your accomplice access for your social media payments and devices or permitting them to tune you via your mobile phone. You may possibly promise to answer your smartphone each time they call and located it on speaker in case you're in a scenario in that you in truth can't speak, in order to concentrate you're telling the fact. Whatever techniques you install region are an excellent manner to determine on however be prepared to do so in choice to actually promising you'll be sincere in destiny.

HOW IMPORTANT IS FULL DISCLOSURE?

If you're going to rebuild your courting after an affair, you're going to need to rebuild receive as genuine with, which by means of way of manner of default approach you need to be honest from right here on in advance. The large question is just how honest you need to be and unfortunately, the jury's out on that one.

Personally, I recommend navigating this manner with the useful useful resource of a licensed therapist you're every cushty with. While the cheated partner merits the solutions to a few factor questions they've got, you furthermore might also need to don't forget whether or not or now not amazing records is actually valuable or whether or not or now not it's going to purpose even more damage. For example, I had one purchaser who demanded her partner tell her in amazing detail about each single intercourse act and then refuse to engage inside the identical acts ever yet again. Unsurprisingly, that courting ended up inside the divorce courts.

Then there were sports wherein the cheater has been open and honest approximately everything they did, sharing the facts so they could keep their marriage, pleasant to have their companion's divorce criminal expert use all that facts in opposition to them.

It's a totally difficult line to stroll.

Each couple is one-of-a-type and the amount of detail required will rely upon a selection of factors, which incorporates whether or not or now not there's any ability for violence, any highbrow fitness problems, your social or religious history, and person type. This is why I paintings with couples on an individual basis to decide the splendid technique for them.

One manner to address the state of affairs is for the cheater to put together a disclosure document with the help in their therapist to provide their companion all of the records about what took place. The wronged birthday party can offer you with a listing of questions about what they've located out, yet again with the help of their therapist, who can assist them decide whether or not a query is vital or whether or no longer or not it's likely to motive greater damage.

For instance, asking, "Did you risk my health?" may be very essential, specifically considering quite a few human beings having extramarital intercourse don't use safety. On the opportunity hand, inquiring for intimate data approximately what exactly went on inside the mattress room is not going to serve any real cause besides there have been gift sexual troubles within the dating.

For a few human beings, giving too much statistics have to do greater damage than appropriate. For others, too little will incredible leave them obsessing over what they don't recognize.

When you are telling your partner about your affair, be thoughtful in their feelings and show regret. Don't interest on how a superb deal a laugh it became and what shape of you loved being with the alternative individual. Be direct. This goes to harm. There's no getting round that. Be organized to reply some thing questions your partner has, and don't forget that at this stage, the future of your dating all hinges on how the dishonest accomplice handles topics. Avoid being protective and attempt to stay as actual as you may. Finally, express regret unconditionally without looking for or stressful forgiveness at this factor. That will come at the same time as the time is proper.

If you're the simplest who become cheated on, try and be strong as you listen and try to understand what you're hearing. Try no longer to move at the assault or look at this device as an possibility to punish your associate for what they've done to you. Talk the whole lot thru. If you're immoderate about staying collectively, try to maintain an open thoughts. You receives past this. Understanding what took place to get you into this mess will help you prevent it from going on within the destiny. Both of you can possibly need to make changes, but inside the long term, this can make you each happier and avoid any need to cheat all over again.

When you've worked via the questions in remedy, you can then draw a line below what happened and work inside the path of what you're going to do in any other case within the future. While it's probably that other questions can also upward push up in the future—which should always be spoke back—while you've worked via the enjoy with a therapist, you may put your interest on wherein it's supposed to be—your courting rather than an affair.

Sharing the story of the affair stops the wronged celebration from turning personal investigator. If they've got all of the statistics they want, they may grieve what happened after which begin to choose up the quantities. This is the first step in the course of healing and saving the marriage.

THE OBSESSION CYCLE

It is very common for a person who has been cheated directly to fall into what's known as the obsession cycle. This is when they sense damage by way of the use of what's took place, simply so they ask questions they've requested previously, attempting new statistics. When they don't get a fantastic solution, they get angry or dissatisfied and withdraw. Their obsession builds until their harm turns into overwhelming, and the cycle starts offevolved offevolved all all another time.

If you find out your self asking the identical questions again and again, you're caught up within the obsession cycle. It's natural to expect that more information will assist heal the ache, and every so often it'll. But if it's miles taking vicinity too lengthy, it will become a way of you keeping off actively processing your harm and looking deeper into what you need to do to rebuild your relationship.

I discover that journaling in truth allows with this method. You can appearance over it and word if there are any recurring topics. Once you've diagnosed them, ask your self if you knew all the solutions, would it now not no longer in fact alternate something? Would it assist you technique your emotions so that you have to flow into on?

Maybe, perhaps no longer.

Using your magazine to write down out your anger and grief approach you aren't continuously bombarding your partner with the equal questions, an amazing manner to subsequently bring about resentment. You'll be able to start processing what's happened and could have a report you can appearance over to appearance the way you've changed and feature a observe which you have superior, even though it doesn't experience like it.

THE DEPRESSION CYCLE

Another functionality pitfall is the depression cycle. It's natural to revel in depressed whilst you're managing the aftermath of being cheated on. This results in you feeling sorry for yourself, as you observe how the affair has negatively impacted you. But you then definately begin to enjoy sorry to your partner, as you take a look at how they're struggling with the impact of their affair. This outcomes in you feeling irritated with yourself for feeling sorry for a person who's harm you so badly, which brings you decrease lower back to depression.

When you've been cheated on, you could discover your self cycling thru all forms of feelings. You keep in mind your self, how hard accomplished via you're, how unfair all of it's far, and the manner angry you're collectively collectively together with your associate. But then you definately definately endure in mind them. You start to see their facet of the story. You look for excuses for his or her conduct and reflect onconsideration on strategies to justify their behavior. This cycle continues, taking you on a real rollercoaster of emotions.

These feelings and mind are a herbal part of processing what's befell. But some people get stuck proper proper here and might't seem to interrupt loose.

You may probably get stuck inside the anger a part of the approach, in case you want to result in bitterness and resentment. If a few thing happens inside the destiny to cause reminiscences of what's took place, that anger will come flooding returned. It can bring about unwanted conduct, which can be fairly self-damaging.

Alternatively, you'll probably get stuck at the opportunity thing of the cycle, looking for reasons to excuse away what occurred. This can bring about you shutting down your feelings or feeling depressed. When you positioned a wall up amongst yourself and people round you, you can't locate your manner once more to the love you as quickly as shared. You enjoy even greater depressed, and the effect in your dating makes topics worse.

Allow yourself to sense angry and unhappy. This is the only manner to process your feelings and circulate beyond them. However, don't allow the ones feelings be an excuse to cope with your partner badly. Talk about your emotions rather than bottle them up, in spite of the fact that they don't seem to make enjoy. You experience the way you sense, and that's k. Try to empathize along aspect your spouse. You'll each have feelings about what passed off, and that they'll likely be more comparable than you realise. Reconnecting will allow you to paintings through them collectively.

A GUIDE TO COMPLETE HONESTY

Earlier in this bankruptcy, we touched upon disclosing the statistics of your affair on your accomplice. Doing this the right way demonstrates that you remorse what happened and are devoted to putting in the try to heal your courting. This is the time to place your partner's desires in advance than your very personal, however you'll need to do it right in case you're going a great manner to flow beforehand.

Write it down. When you first start discussing what took place, feelings are going to be strolling immoderate. Writing it out lets in you to take a step decrease again, recollect precisely the way you want to give an reason for topics and go through in mind how plenty element to encompass. You can also take a while over the record to make sure you've remembered the whole lot important.

Having a written file allows your partner to get a easy image of what took place, and they'll be able to pass over it over again inside the event that they need to get statistics they'll have not noted the primary time round. It furthermore allows you to consciousness on the difficulty to be had in preference to getting element-tracked within the warm temperature of the immediately.

Keep the point of interest for your personal conduct/moves. Write approximately what befell, wherein, whilst, and with whom.

Don't get caught up in emotions or flowery descriptions.

Share your thoughts and motivations. It's important to be honest approximately the manner you justified your affair to your self with out passing the blame in your associate. Ultimately, you chose to have an affair while you could have made top notch picks. The obligation remains yours. But you may write some issue like: "I changed into feeling . . . However I understand now which have turn out to be no excuse."

Share your feelings. It's clean to anticipate your companion isn't inquisitive about your emotions and that the nice difficulty you could do is pay attention to them speak approximately theirs. In truth, both your feelings are legitimate and vital. When you percentage the way you feel, you're establishing up and being inclined, this is just what your companion wishes once they're feeling prone themselves.

Write about how your infidelity has affected you and those around you. When you're stuck up in an affair, you're not often considering how it's going to impact those spherical you. If you probable did, you probable wouldn't have had an affair within the first place. At the very least, it might have taken away a number of the fun and pleasure. Now is the time to reflect on the quantity of the harm you've finished.

Strive for the right amount of element. Too loads facts is overwhelming and may be hurtful. Too little can make it appear to be you're however in search of to hide a few component. Consider writing some aspect like this:

We met for the first time even as you had taken the kids to visit your parents for the weekend. We went to a neighborhood hotel as it felt incorrect to carry her back to our domestic. She booked and paid for a room at the motel down the road from my administrative center. After you left, I referred to as her to get the information of our room and drove to the motel. We had unprotected intercourse. I determined not to spend the night time because it felt too intimate. As fast as it modified into over, I regretted it.

THE DOS AND DON'TS OF CONFESSING TO AN AFFAIR

Do paintings with a therapist. This is going to be the only way of supporting you every deal with all of the sturdy feelings you'll be experiencing to discover a manner in advance.

Don't revel in you have to recognize all the information proper away. While you'll probably experience together with you need to apprehend everything the second you find out, it can not be the tremendous time to get the solution to all your questions. Given time, you will likely discover you don't need or need to realize the entirety.

Do percent the first-class amount of detail. As we've simply noted, an excessive amount of or too little records can be negative. Sharing intimate, image information might be impossible to transport beyond. Discuss with a therapist first in case you're unsure whether or no longer you need to talk about a few problem.

Don't sense like you need to make a desire right now. When you find out about an affair, the future can seem unsure. Know that you don't must decide something right away. We rarely make right alternatives while we're feeling crushed. Take the time to reflect onconsideration on it, communicate the scenario with a few relied on human beings, and don't forget your alternatives.

Do inform the fact. It's everyday to need to lie after an affair has been determined, either brazenly or thru the usage of omission. When a person is panicked and doesn't want to lose their spouse, it's herbal to bypass over positive topics or lie due to the reality they're frightened of the consequences. Trust me. Things received't get any worse however lying approximately it'll in fact make it worse.

Don't drip feed statistics. Make superb you tell your associate all the important information in advance. Telling them a part of the tale, then a few days later revealing a little greater and then a touch extra a few days after so that it will go away your partner feeling insecure and on location, searching beforehand to the subsequent little little bit of horrible statistics. This is why a disclosure record written with the steerage of a therapist can be so precious. It receives everything out inside the open proper from the start.

Do pick out the proper time and region to show your affair. Ideally, the superb manner to cope with the overall disclosure of an affair is with the help of a certified counselor. If this isn't possible, don't forget carefully while and wherein could be the maximum suitable.

Don't communicate the information:

In the the front of children.

While below the have an impact on of alcohol or tablets.

Late at night time time time.

In public (which embody at artwork, over social media, at church, and so forth.).

Via text, e-mail, or cellphone.

In a car.

EXERCISES

These are some sporting sports activities you can do together at the side of your companion to begin the system of strolling thru infidelity. Ideally, find out a therapist that will help you through the ones physical sports, but if this isn't possible for something cause, find an appropriate time and location to do them so you can art work via them at your personal tempo.

The Honesty after an Affair Exercise

1. Create a listing of questions

Write down each single element you've been trying to invite your companion approximately their affair. Then circulate over every query and ask yourself whether or not or now not you actually need to realize the solution? What distinction will the answer make to you? Will the reality assist or damage you? Will you obsess over the answers you get, or will it hassle you greater to no longer ask the query? If you are every dedicated to saving your dating, are the solutions even though critical?

2. Create a steady vicinity to get honest answers

Your associate needs to revel in robust enough to speak in confidence to you with the solutions on your questions. This calls as a way to stay calm in an effort to inform you matters they will be afraid of exposing.

Remember, your associate is best human. They made a mistake, but they're in search of to position it proper. Try to live on top of factors of your emotional reactions and take a break if it all will become an excessive amount of. You're probable to listen a few matters which can make you want to retaliate. You want to live on top of these urges. Behaving erratically, terrible-mouthing your associate to friends and own family or contacting the possibility female/man will only cause more harm in your relationship.

You may additionally observe topics that make you question whether or not the damage for your dating can ever be repaired. Consider that your partner might be feeling the equal way. Make a promise to yourself and your companion that you'll do your fantastic to art work via a few element comes up. It also can sense which includes you acquired't live in this manner in the warmness of the immediately, but I've seen couples come via seemingly not feasible situations and be closer than ever.

3. Ask your questions

Once you've finalized your list of have-to-apprehend questions, it's time for you to ask them. Your accomplice wants to be geared up to offer sincere answers, no matter how difficult it is probably. They need to be committed to appearing with compassion in the direction of you, giving you the reassurance you want to live collectively and rebuild accept as true with. Supporting each one in all a type through this method is a effective way to supply you closer collectively and start you on the road to recuperation.

Always maintain in thoughts that the purpose is to apprehend what happened, not advantage ammunition to apply closer to the possibility. For this to art work, you want to accept that during a few unspecified time inside the destiny you'll need to region this inside the past, even if you're no longer organized to carry out that right now. Working together as a set, you can repair what changed into damaged.

Writing a Full Disclosure

We've mentioned the importance of a written complete disclosure. It's time with the intention to located pen to paper and write a number one draft. The following questions will help you get your mind out. Not all the questions is probably applicable for your instances, so use the ones you want and forget about approximately the relaxation. You should probable like to transport over your disclosure with a therapist earlier than sharing it collectively with your partner. You can also write the solutions to every query on separate quantities of paper to move away vicinity for observe-up questions from your therapist, obligation partner, or associate.

Objectification. When did you first word your self rating humans with the resource in their physical appearance? Did you experience an enchantment toward tremendous traits or strengths? How did you begin rearranging your lifestyles to encounter, locate want with, or keep away from human beings you determined appealing? How did those adjustments make you feel isolated or fake? How did it lead you to begin preserving secrets and techniques and strategies or telling lies?

Physical lust. What are the most attractive functions in the contrary sex? What locations or sports activities did you've got interaction in to area yourself within the manner of temptation? How did you arrange it slow so you can be around attractive people?

Lustful thoughts. What romantic or erotic subjects do you discover yourself considering the most? What goals or insecurities do those address? What movies or books encapsulate those troubles? How lots time do you spend watching or studying the ones? How an entire lot time do you spend fantasizing approximately those issues?

Soft porn. What become your first revel in with smooth porn? What is your cutting-edge experience with it? Do you sexualize any elements of your modern-day lifestyles, in order that they mimic clean porn? Do you've got any rituals to prepare yourself for mild porn? What triggers a desire to bask in slight porn? Do you use sexual hobby as a reward for your self?

Hard porn. What modified into your first exposure to tough porn? How lots time do you spend looking at porn every week? How a splendid deal coins have you ever ever spent on it? Do you have any modern-day-day subscriptions? Do you've got pornography hidden everywhere, each physical or electronically? Do you've got got were given any mystery e mail money owed?

Anonymous interactions. Do you use any web websites, cellphone strains, or specific offerings to connect with special people for the abilities of sexual interest? Do you operate any chat rooms, social networking web sites or matchmaking services? How lots time do you spend searching out a person to engage with? Are your real call and make contact with records listed everywhere? Have you despatched pics of your self (sexual or otherwise) or communicated over webcam? As you get to apprehend someone via any of these techniques, do you sense your self becoming greater attracted or much less fascinated? Have you ever scheduled a assembly with each person?

Emotional affairs. How did the relationship start, and while did the conversations bypass the road? What horrible statements have you ever ever made about your spouse or marriage? Have you informed each exceptional you're attracted? Do you've got had been given any manner of hidden communique? When, wherein, and how do you talk? How have you ever ever hidden this out of your partner? How smooth is it to cover the relationship? Do you bypass on dates? Was your conduct driven by means of way of way of a sense of sadness to your modern-day-day courting or appeal to this new individual?

Sexual contact with out intercourse. Did you hold palms, massage each specific, hug, kiss, take away your apparel, fondle every particular or interact in oral intercourse? How many human beings have you ever ever completed this with? With every person, how typically? With everyone over how extended? What stopped you from taking the next step?

One-off sexual encounter. How many humans have you ever ever had one-off encounters with? Who pursued whom? Did you intentionally located your self in temptation's way? Is there a opportunity of pregnancy from any of those encounters? Have you paid for intercourse? Were alcohol or pills worried?

Affairs. In addition to answering the questions round emotional affairs, write about at the same time as the sex commenced. What percentage of your interactions with the opportunity character was sexual? Did you're making any expressions of love or dedication? (Verbal, devices, journeys, and so forth.) Was it a romantic relationship or extra like friends with blessings? Who else knew approximately the relationship?

Longer-time period affairs. What plans did you are making to go away your partner? Did you do any research or prepare any movement steps? Did you introduce any circle of relatives, buddies, or kids to your different partner? Did you protect your unique associate emotionally or financially on the fee of your first partner and family? What lies did you inform your self or others to justify your picks?

Full Disclosure Follow-Up for the Betrayed Partner

After you've heard your companion's whole disclosure, make the effort to mirror on what you've determined. You'll have greater question and probable want to make clean sure statistics. Asking the ones on every occasion they pop into your thoughts will make it more tough so one can assimilate everything you're recommended, and it could undermine the sensitive trust you're seeking to rebuild. What's more, random questions get random answers which can purpose paranoia, even in case your partner is being honest.

Keep a pocket book to be had and write down questions every time they arrive up. Do this for a few days after which put together them. This will assist you be aware your companion's solutions as part of a cohesive entire, making it a whole lot much less difficult as a manner to understand what they're pronouncing.

You can set up your questions in a number of techniques:

Based on the whole disclosure outline.

Based at the data of your marriage/timeline of the affair.

Based on the numerous topics.

Based on the feelings on the again of every query.

As an entire lot as you desperately may moreover want to recognize why, this is the fine query I may additionally suggest closer to asking due to the reality there aren't any particular answers. Either the solution seems like your spouse is blaming you for no longer gratifying their desires, or they in truth haven't any idea, to be able to make you experience angry. Instead, are searching out to invite questions that will help you come to terms with what's befell.

If you revel in that your accomplice isn't being honest, tell them the manner you're feeling. Ask them what they could do to be more apparent so that you can start to take transport of as true with them all over again.

I suggest in opposition to playing detective without your companion's consent—this may handiest undermine the receive as proper with you're seeking to assemble. Do no longer do whatever illegal at the same time as looking to get to the heart of the hassle, and don't permit your desperation to find out the reality grow to be an obsession. Work with a therapist so that you can located any fears or concerns into the right context.

In this economic catastrophe, we've regarded deeply at the problem of honesty. You've positioned out about:

Why humans lie after an affair.

The importance of being honest and the way you'll be in reality open about what you've carried out.

The obsession and depression cycles.

The dos and don'ts approximately discussing your affair.

Full disclosure and the way you could prepare your private report.

I can't strain enough how critical honesty is to get over an affair. If you don't sense you're going in case you need to be honest, you have to ask yourself a few extreme questions on the future of your courting. Why are you terrified of being sincere? You can't do any greater damage than you have already got. Being dishonest is what got you right proper right here in the first place. It's time to strive a one in all a kind manner.

Chapter 3: Grief

I diplomatically positioned the box of tissues inside the path of the sobbing female sitting opposite me.

"It's actually so difficult, you understand? We've been collectively for over thirty years. I've constantly loved my husband. We've had 3 youngsters together. Sure, we've had hard times, but I've usually been there to assist him. When he out of region his method, I emerge as there for him, letting him recognize I wasn't with him for his cash. I cherished him like I've by no means loved every person else. And now I've found out that he's been having an affair for the past 5 years with a girl an entire lot more youthful than him. What am I supposed to do with that? Thirty years of marriage lengthy long beyond due to the fact he couldn't maintain it in his pants. I experience like I don't recognise who he's. I don't realize who I am. It's like my entire life is a lie, and I don't apprehend what to do.

I've misplaced the whole lot. It's like my husband's died, high-quality he's nevertheless right right here, although hurting me."

She broke down over again, and all I may also moreover need to do became sympathize. When you discover your accomplice has been cheating on you, grief is one of the maximum commonplace reactions. You'll want to absolutely grieve the lack of the relationship you concept you had earlier than you can go along with the drift on. Grief is a hard emotion and one that few people absolutely recognize. It's outstanding for each person. How you enjoy is how you experience.

HOW LONG WILL IT TAKE FOR ME TO RECOVER FROM MY SPOUSE'S AFFAIR?

While each circumstance is specific, that is a tough timeline for the recuperation approach:

Zero to Six Weeks

This is the immediately aftermath of finding out about the affair while putting in place what befell. You'll be feeling stunned, with feelings flying everywhere in the location. Ideally, with the useful resource of the surrender of six weeks, the entire tale has come out, so that you can drift on to the next degree. If now not, it'll be more difficult an excellent manner to rebuild accept as true with.

Six Months

This is in that you want to go through severa actions so you can each revel in solid in transferring earlier to your dating. You want to sense your associate even though cares and can be grieving the shortage of the relationship you concept you had. They want to be doing some component is essential to provide you the peace of thoughts it gained't occur once more. You'll both want to discover the tale inside the again of why it passed off.

Nine to Twelve Months

This is even as you'll find out yourself feeling prepared to forgive, on the manner to allow you to certainly reconcile. You each want to have a smooth photo of why the affair took place, and your partner have to have been strolling on themselves and reassuring you that they're really devoted for your marriage.

Twelve to Eighteen Months

Now you'll be ready to determine to transport on together. Your courting might also have modified, but hopefully for the better. You'll have observed out the way you cope with adversity collectively and advanced better techniques of speaking.

If the idea of your current state of affairs happening for eighteen months is a supply of stress, please try now not to fear approximately it. If you're every putting in the time and energy, you'll see enhancements a incredible deal in advance than that. It's clearly that, in my enjoy, this is extra or much less the amount of time it takes to completely technique your feelings about the affair.

FORGIVENESS

I often pay hobby customers say, "If they could actually forgive me, we can also additionally want to get beyond this." They appear to think that forgiveness is a magic wand they may be able to wave to make everything right. As I'm sure you're conscious, it doesn't in fact art work like that.

I need to make it very smooth what forgiveness is not:

Forgiveness is not ignoring your feelings. Just due to the fact you forgive a person doesn't suggest you aren't still hurting.

Forgiveness doesn't advocate the whole thing's ok. It doesn't let your associate justify what they did or escape without any outcomes.

Forgiveness doesn't excuse topics. It doesn't absolve your companion of responsibility for what they did.

Forgiveness isn't forgetting. You can't wipe the slate clean sincerely with the resource of announcing you're sorry.

Forgiveness doesn't repair accept as true with. It's step one within the path of trusting, but it's no longer the whole tale.

Forgiveness doesn't equate reconciliation. You can forgive a person and nevertheless in no manner want to deal with them all over again.

Put sincerely, forgiveness is freeing yourself from the affair's maintain over you. It's deciding on to allow yourself glide on in desire to obsessing over what took place and permitting it to form your destiny behavior. It is a few aspect you could do without the person who's wronged you ever doing anything. As lots as it's first rate while someone says sorry or attempts to make amends, sometimes that's really not possible. You however have the electricity to forgive them.

There are 3 steps to forgiveness:

1.   Acknowledging the harm, in this situation, that an affair has passed off.

2.   Admitting that amends need to be made, that some detail wants to be performed to make up for that harm.

3.   Releasing the alternative celebration from the need to make amends.

It's flawlessly herbal to want your partner to do some thing to make subjects proper. We've already referred to some of those options. But whilst you forgive them, you choose now not to allow what they do have any electricity over you. Regardless of whether or not or no longer you make a decision to stay together or not, you allow yourself to transport directly to a brighter future.

If you enjoy that you can't forgive your partner, that's appropriate enough. It's normal to take a while on the manner to allow pass of past hurts. You must be conscious that at the same time as you don't forgive someone, it could effect your bodily, emotional, and religious fitness. In truth, at the identical time as you forgive someone, it has nothing to do with making matters simpler for them and the entirety to do with making things better for you.

You can forgive someone and still set up vicinity obstacles and techniques to make sure they gained't repeat the conduct in the future. Fool me as quick as, shame on you; idiot me two times, disgrace on me.

But in case you're excessive approximately rebuilding your dating, you're going to need to discover ways to agree with all over again. And that can first-class come after you've forgiven them.

GRIEF

Recovering from betrayal is a manner akin to grieving after a bereavement. You've out of place the spouse you perception you had. You've misplaced the wedding you perception you had. You've out of place your self-picture of someone who knew their accomplice interior and out. So many losses—of path, you're going to want to grieve.

Grief is a noticeably misunderstood emotion. It's a deep struggling that movements us to our very core and expresses itself in excellent tactics. When a person you like betrays you, it feels like the ultimate non-public attack. What's greater, you don't get the same degree of guide you could have if your associate had died. There's no formal ritual that will help you in pronouncing goodbye to the past. Nobody rallies spherical to attend to you. Instead, you're imagined to surely recover from it or get out—there's no gray place.

Grief is an inner system in place of mourning, this is the external expression of grief. Grief have to make one sense numb, unhappy, irritated, regretful or perhaps relieved, at the same time as mourning may contain speakme, crying, or lashing out. Mourning allows you to approach your grief, this is why it's so crucial to allow yourself to mourn in the manner that is healthiest and maximum useful for you.

Recognize that you've been damage very badly. The ache runs deep. It's not a few issue you'll in reality get over in a few weeks or perhaps months. If you're locating yourself though suffering to transport on and it's been a long time, say, ten months, ask your self, if my accomplice had died, should I though be suffering? Chances are, you'd solution positive.

You've been via a similar bereavement with dropping the character you concept you knew. Allow yourself time and be kind to your self.

Self-care following a betrayal

The most important trouble whilst getting higher from an affair is to be type to your self.

Express your grief. Your feelings may be unpredictable and excessive in the course of this era. This is normal. Giving your self permission to in truth sense and art work on the side of your emotions rather than bottling them up will help you method them that a bargain faster.

Don't blame your self. It's easy accountable your self for what passed off, mainly if you be by using manner of low shallowness. You can start telling yourself you're the handiest answerable for the infidelity because you weren't able to meet your partner's wishes in some component manner. Alternatively, you is probably indignant with your self for not information some thing have become incorrect faster. Beating yourself up over what befell won't help you heal. If you discover your self having those kinds of thoughts, provide you with opposite statements to restrict the damage. E.G., in case you find out your self wondering, I need to have spent greater time with him, counter it with I spent as hundreds time as I want to have. He have to have made greater time for me. His affair isn't my fault.

Look after yourself. Infidelity can bring about hypervigilance and worry that your companion will cheat another time in case you don't do in reality everything they need. Neglecting your desires to make a person else happy isn't sustainable and obtained't maintain your marriage.

Don't make any maximum crucial alternatives. When we make choices at some point of instances of emotional turmoil, we rarely make proper options.

Don't make any knee-jerk reactions. You may additionally determine you may't stay together with your partner, however don't make that choice immediately (until your partner is abusive). Give it a while earlier than you make a decision to do some issue you may later regret.

Don't isolate your self. You may revel in disgrace or humiliation that your accomplice has cheated on you, preventing you from achieving out to someone for help. You may additionally discover that you don't always get the aid you need. If you visit a chum, as an example, they will urge you to leave your companion whilst you want to paintings in your marriage, this is why it's exceptional to discover someone who may be intention—collectively with a therapist. You may also need to research useful resource companies, every in person or on-line. While those aren't right for certainly absolutely everyone, many human beings discover it beneficial to percentage their mind and testimonies with folks which can be going thru what they're going via. You even make new pals.

How to grieve

The manner we grieve is fashioned via many elements, which encompass how your circle of relatives treated emotion, your revel in of loss, your person and gender, your lifestyle, and whether or not you will be inclined to be a fact seeker, feeler, or doer. Grieving doesn't observe a inflexible layout and doesn't usually have a step-through-step sample.

You can also have heard of the Kübler-Ross five degrees of grief: denial, anger, bargaining, despair, and reputation. You can also furthermore even recognize them in your self. I favor to use J. William Worden's model of dealing with grief in obligations because it allows my customers to be more proactive when it comes to working thru their grief.

The first venture

Accept that you have suffered a loss. Common feelings are surprise, numbness, and disbelief. Initially, this could make you appear strong whilst sincerely you're indifferent from your feelings. When your feelings come flooding again after the numbness wears off, it may be overwhelming.

The second assignment

Once you've familiar the dearth of your preceding marriage, it's time to paintings thru the ache of grief. This challenge can comprise you experiencing a huge range of emotions, along with sadness, tension, anger, isolation, loneliness, guilt, and treatment. You can also even revel in which include you're going loopy due to the fact your feelings are so unstable. Be affected man or woman with your self, and don't be afraid to get expert resource as you undergo this.

How to narrate for your companion after an affair

You might also determine it might be a remarkable concept to brief separate after an affair. This will provide you with on every occasion to approach and adjust. Ask yourself whether or not or no longer you may live underneath the same roof with out verbally or maybe bodily attacking each unique. Question whether you may address seeing your associate each day in your cutting-edge emotional state. This will inform you whether or not or no longer you must take some time apart.

There are one-of-a-kind options if you decide to in brief separate. Separating and drowsing in specific regions of the home and averting every distinctive as an entire lot as feasible may be the first-rate opportunity if you want to present yourselves the risk to paintings to your problems, lessen the effect to your youngsters and limit the financial effect of a separation. One of you quick moving out is probably a better choice in case you can not assure every other's emotional or bodily protection, if the betrayed associate can't undergo to be round the other and if the cheater isn't prepared to make amends or get help.

In the preliminary aftermath of an affair, couples often change between having lengthy, immoderate fights, and appearing as even though no longer some thing has passed off, refusing to talk approximately the affair. Neither approach is particularly inexperienced, that is why looking for help from an authorized therapist is a remarkable idea to begin a healthy dialog.

Some couples are unsure whether or not they want to be having intercourse. Ultimately, this is all the manner all the way down to the individual couple. Realistically, it comes proper right down to whether or now not being intimate will be useful or unhelpful. The very last selection need to constantly lie with the betrayed spouse. At a few point, you'll need to renew sexual own family members, however at the same time as that point comes will depend upon you.

It's ordinary now not to want to have any sexual touch. It's additionally regular to experience a heightened sex force as a manner to reconnect at the aspect of your partner. Be conscious that those emotions can change at any again and again; that is flawlessly normal. Listen to your self and apprehend the way you experience.

I'd strongly advise you to get your self examined for the complete spectrum of sexually transmitted ailments, even if your companion says it's useless. STDs are commonplace and do now not want complete sex for a person to be infected. Be secure and make certain you're both uninfected.

Relearning the way to talk collectively along with your accomplice

I've stated it in advance than, and I'm going to replicate it earlier than this book is completed: conversation is pinnacle to enhancing from a betrayal. The one element the cheater and the cheated on normally have in commonplace is they don't feel heard. Emotions cloud your wondering, and also you get so stuck up for your very personal ache which you conflict to be aware of all people else's. It doesn't take masses for subjects to start out evenly high-quality to unexpectedly descend into yelling, stopping, screaming, and tears. If you don't recognize how to talk to each other without getting out of place like this, your problems can't ever be resolved, and you'll in no way rebuild your relationship. This is why getting manual from a therapist is that this form of correct idea—they may train you new strategies of speaking, together with:

Imago communication. This is a three-step tool advanced by using way of the use of Harville Hendrix, Ph.D. And Helen LaKelly

Hunt, Ph.D. The steps are mirroring, validation, and empathy. It technique you take some time to recognize what your companion is telling you before thinking about your private reaction. It teaches you to apprehend your accomplice's experience on the identical time as now not having to compromise your non-public.

Emotion-targeted treatment. This approach teaches you the manner to apprehend what your companion's emotions are telling you. So, as an instance, if a few component takes area to remind your associate of your betrayal, rather of getting aggravated with them for being upset, you could widely recognized that they're feeling damage proper now and encourage them to percentage what they're going through with you. By validating your partner's feelings, you show you care and are satisfied to help them heal. It can be tough to try this while you enjoy your associate's emotional response is an attack, however it in reality can deliver you together.

Monologs. Sometimes it's hard for a pair to interact in a regular once more-and-forth communication. With the monolog method, you agree on a difficult and speedy quantity of time for one man or woman to talk at the same time as the opportunity individual listens and takes notes. You then take a smash, possibly even leaving it to day after today to go back to the state of affairs. This permits you to sense heard with out being interrupted.

Keeping a diary. Writing things out is a great way of exploring your feelings about the affair. It's a form of personal communication which lets in you to examine the situation with a superb amount of emotional distance. Writing helps you to slow down and mirror on what's taking place so you can studies greater about who you're and what you need. Keep your diary in a personal and safe vicinity so you apprehend you may write with out fear of your terms causing any harm need to a person else examine them.

Write a letter. This can be in the shape of a disclosure letter, which we've stated in the remaining monetary destroy. A letter allows you to take the time to carefully bear in mind the phrases you pick out and the way you need to talk. Some humans discover that the clean act of writing a letter is all they want, and they don't deliver it to the supposed recipient.

Emotional triggers at a few stage inside the grieving technique

Emotional triggers are intrusive feelings and mind surrounding the affair. Your apprehensive system is going into overdrive, reacting to the situation as a risk. You enjoy a surge of adrenaline as your frame prepares to cope with the danger. Once this has befell, then the prefrontal cortex (the part of the mind controlling reasoning and better-degree concept) will have a look at whether or not or now not or not you're virtually in chance.

Triggers are not:

A way of punishing the cheater.

A signal of unforgiveness.

A profound notion into your partner or the scenario. (We might also moreover furthermore experience the thoughts we've got while we're in this heightened kingdom are smooth even as, in fact, they may be heavily prompted thru our emotions.)

A setback.

In reality, triggers are an opportunity to do some more recovery and reconnect collectively together with your partner.

If you are the pleasant who cheated:

Approach your spouse with compassion and mild hobby. It is your mission now to understand and resource your partner. This involves accepting your very personal shame and guilt over the scenario.

Do now not keep away from your associate's ache. It's hard to cope with a person else's pain, especially at the same time as you're the one who delivered about it. But this could make your accomplice experience even more abandoned and by myself. Be willing to be there for them once they're dealing with a purpose or supply them vicinity if that's what they want.

See the harm and fear within the back of the anger. Your companion's anger is coming from an area of ache. When you may do not forget that, it makes it much less difficult to stay calm.

Conversation starters need to involve things like:

Help me understand how I hurt you.

I'm not going anywhere. I'm proper proper right here for you.

I'm going to paintings with you to understand why this befell.

I'll answer any questions, even if you've already asked them.

It's ok to speak about [the trigger] as an entire lot as you want.

What are you feeling proper now?

If you're the only who grow to be cheated on:

Understand that triggers are an opportunity as a manner to system your ache. You don't want to feel the manner you do, but it's far what it's far. Processing your pain allows you to transport via it in choice to burying it, so it maintains to understand-out you.

Talk about the cause. This will assist you approach what's going on so that you can heal.

Make effective you get compassion and care from your partner. It's important that you feel they care about what you're going thru and help you even as you're suffering.

Put plans in place so you can actively see your partner running to decide out why they did what they did. They want to demonstrate they're willing to private as plenty as what they did, take transport of the effects and analyze greater approximately themselves.

I offer my clients a five-step approach to paintings via triggers:

1. Acknowledge what's took place

If you're the betrayed associate, pay interest while you're being triggered, at the equal time as you apprehend the onset of a added approximately reaction. Be kind to your self. Let your self revel in the feelings in preference to trying to bury them.

If you're the cheater, don't inform your accomplice that they're being delivered approximately. Instead, resource them thru their emotions and don't inform them to save you feeling the manner they do. Tell them you're right right here for them and willing to be aware about some factor they want to say.

2. Identify the reason

If you're the betrayed accomplice, bear in mind whether or no longer or now not you're responding to a modern danger, which includes your partner being secretive, seeking to make you experience responsible or becoming protective, or whether or no longer or not you're reacting to a memory. This will help you are making feel of what's happening and what you need to do to similarly manner the affair.

If you're the cheater, recollect the manner you're feeling on this 2d. If you're getting irritated, it's likely that this is protecting underlying guilt and disgrace. Notice in case you locate yourself getting protecting, aggressive or manipulative to avoid managing your shame and guilt and paintings to be more supportive of your spouse.

3. Ask for what you want

If you're the betrayed partner, bear in mind what is probably maximum useful for you right now. Do you need to talk to someone, be thru yourself, or spend time together with your associate or a pal? Don't be afraid to mention what you want after which offer it to yourself.

If you're the cheater, be aware of what your accomplice desires and do your extremely good to give it to them, although it method answering the identical questions all over again. Appreciate that your companion isn't being intentionally provocative or unforgiving. They are honestly going via the restoration way.

four. What to do even as you talk

If you're the betrayed associate, don't use threats to get your element at some stage in, which includes pronouncing you'll leave or have an affair of your non-public. If you observe thru, it'll only purpose more damage. Telling your associate, "You've sincerely damage me," is greater powerful than "I want to sleep with a person else, so you understand how this feels."

If you're the cheater, maintain your awareness on your partner's emotions in vicinity of yours. Don't say such things as: "I'm sorry" or "I need I'd finished subjects in a one among a kind way." This maintains the spotlight on you. Instead, reflect lower back in your accomplice what they're telling you. This permits them to apprehend you care about their emotions.

5. Be grateful for the triggers

While they're unsightly, triggers are an possibility to take a protracted have a take a look at ourselves and our relationship without rose-colored glasses to see what's definitely going on. They carry up severa trash, but that is a risk to clean it out as quickly as and for all.

When you ask, "What do I need to do?" you could flow ahead together on your recuperation adventure.

Who to speak to approximately the affair

It's a fantastic concept to be discerning whom you speak the affair with. Before locating out whom to talk to approximately the affair, think cautiously approximately whether or not or now not someone is stable or risky.

Safe human beings:

Give you unconditional love and popularity.

Can sit down down with your grief in area of telling you to move on or try and distract you from it.

Don't gossip.

Don't attempt to repair matters or deliver answers.

Can cope with irritated outbursts and sturdy feelings.

Understand that we're all human and fallacious.

Offer love in desire to advice.

Unsafe people:

Play the blame game.

Deny what's took place or lower it.

Try to recuperation the situation.

Give undesirable advice.

Gossip.

Are most effective there for you if you're happy and aren't going via a difficult time.

Are conceited or self-righteous.

Once you've identified actual human beings to talk to, ask them to go to lunch or have a coffee with you. Tell them you've were given subjects taking vicinity and you'd like to speak approximately it with them. Tell them what you want from them. So if you're searching out a sounding board, tell them that. Likewise, permit them to understand if you do or don't need their recommendation and allow them to apprehend if you're working with a therapist, genuinely so that they don't must take on that feature.

Not everybody wants to recognise what's befell but having a few supportive people round you who are aware of the info may be sincerely beneficial and just what you want to make it thru.

If children are concerned, they need to recognise what's took place, but you need to present the information in a cautious, age-appropriate way. Just as you've taken the time to keep in mind whether or not or not you're going to stay or cross, you should additionally take the time in figuring out at the same time as and the manner to speak on your children.

Don't make guarantees you couldn't be capable of maintain. You could in all likelihood promise that you're now not splitting up, but in case your partner keeps with their affair, you can determine to forestall your marriage. If that occurs, your children can be disillusioned with you for breaking your promise.

Tell your children that you're going thru a difficult time and looking to determine topics out, but you every love them very an lousy lot. "I don't recognize" is a wonderfully applicable solution and is lots much less bad than telling them some aspect which seems to be incorrect further down the street.

You can also like to talk approximately on the aspect of your therapist what to tell your youngsters. And mainly, in no way say some factor derogatory on your youngsters about your accomplice.

Exercises

Couples counseling exercise for infidelity

Answer the following questions together together along with your accomplice:

1. What are the triggers linked to the affair?

2. How do you experience even as you're added on?

As you percent your thoughts about your triggers together along with your partner, be as open and honest as viable to construct closer connections. If you're the handiest taking note of the solutions, don't decide or criticize. Simply ask your partner what you could do to assist them.

Being capable of find out and paintings through triggers will help deliver the 2 of you together. After an affair, it's natural to region up shielding walls which get within the way of constructing bridges. Being open and sincere about your triggers will help convey down those walls.

Put yourself in your companion's shoes

If you're the cheater, sit down and make a list of 40 different things which might also reason your companion. This isn't aimed closer to shaming or condemning your associate for overreacting—quite the opposite. Instead, that could be a way so you can attempt to respect what they're presently going via and the manner you will be extra aware about their triggers and goals. You can then communicate about this together and be aware what you can every do to make your companion revel in more stable and additional solid.

In this bankruptcy, we tested grief. You decided out about:

The timeline of grief.

The power of forgiveness.

Practicing self-care following infidelity.

How to grieve effectively.

Relearning the way to speak.

Triggers and a way to address them.

In the following chapter, we're going to test what you may do to make amends and begin to move past what's happened.

Chapter 4: Making Amends

I looked at the couple sitting at the couch opposite me. "What made you ebook a session with me?" I asked.

They glanced at each specific, each seeming to inspire the alternative to be the number one to talk. At final, the girl, Liz, said, "I had an affair."

I smiled to reassure her. "You're no longer the number one individual to tell me that, and I'm great you received't be the final. What do you desire to accumulate through coming to appearance me?"

"We want to store our marriage," her husband, Mike, informed me. "I propose, I actually need to keep our marriage. I'm absolutely now not fine if it's feasible."

"I'm no longer going to make any guarantees," I said. "But in case you each need to make it work, we are capable of in reality do our nice to determine out what went wrong and see if we are able to positioned it proper."

Over the direction of our time together, we managed to get to the coronary heart of what befell. Liz had misplaced her father at an early age, which left her with emotions of abandonment. She in no way felt nicely sufficient, did everything she notion Mike desired at the fee of her non-public happiness and averted war in any respect prices because of the truth she felt that if she fought with Mike, he'd depart her. Over time, she omitted who she changed into, and due to the reality she'd been so targeted on captivating Mike, she'd unnoticed her non-public goals.

Liz met someone at art work who started flirting with her. She felt like she may be herself with him due to the truth she had no longer something to lose. This feeling of freedom and recognition she expert collectively with her co-employee in the end brought about her having a physical affair.

It took lots of hard work for Liz to recognize how her childhood memories had introduced her to this vicinity. At the same time, Mike wanted a extraordinary deal of help to apprehend how Liz can also need to love him and cheat on him. It took a while, but eventually, he have become capable of see that it become due to the reality she cherished him. She turned into frightened of losing him via being herself, which became part of the motive why she have become to someone else.

Both of them did pretty a few art work on themselves to triumph over their troubles. Mike worked to find out the compassion for Liz's emotions at the equal time as restoration his very own.

A lot of this became pleasant viable because of the fact Liz took complete responsibility for her selections. She worked hard to make amends and rebuild accept as true with together along with her husband. She started out out to speak in confidence to

Mike approximately her thoughts and emotions, while Mike listened and didn't take benefit of her vulnerabilities.

Together, they took the shattered portions of their marriage and reconnected with each specific thru sharing their innermost mind, taking note of each exclusive and consciously selecting to be compassionate and type. While they both could have desired for the affair no longer to have took place, by the time they stopped coming to me, that they had created a marriage that modified into stronger and nearer than something they'd ever experienced previously.

Making amends isn't optionally available

When a person has been hurt, they're more likely to forgive the person who damage them if that character actively takes steps to make amends. Making amends is prime to repairing a courting while you've broken a person's don't forget or damage them. Even in case your partner minimizes your attempts or isn't prepared to truely take delivery of your apology, it's vital you do your exceptional to proper the incorrect. This acknowledges what you've finished and facilitates pave the way to solving things.

When you are making amends, you're accepting duty in your transgressions. The more you may do that without blaming the alternative individual or making excuses, the greater honest your efforts to rebuild the connection will appear.

Be regular

Making amends isn't a shortcut to getting all over again to the way things had been (which isn't possible). It's in reality the first-class way to get lower back heading in the right direction to building a brand new, more splendid courting. This is an extended-term method due to the reality proving you are willing to do matters in each other manner calls for diligent, each day movement that demonstrates you're making a trade. You are selecting to be honest, respectful and humble, and you could fine show this by way of the usage of the use of behaving in a way this is regular and right.

When you decide to make amends, you may want to anticipate it's going to take time to your partner to get over your affair. You may be feeling responsible, shameful, or humiliated, so don't want to talk about the affair or near down the verbal exchange even because it does come up. You need to allow your partner to speak approximately topics as they want in an open, empathic manner. Showing you could take delivery of the blame and address your emotions of guilt or remorse with out reflecting this returned at your associate or walking a long way from the communication will do lots to show you are worth of believe.

You will need to recognize any new rules or regulations your companion wants to hooked up vicinity. After all, they've had been given suitable purpose to be mistrustful of you, so in the event that they want to look your emails, cellphone logs, and so forth., collect that that is how it's far—at the least right now. You've had been given nothing to cover anymore . . . Have you?

Be open to growing any adjustments vital to place your relationship in a higher place. Accept that this may even mean large lifestyles adjustments, together with converting jobs or moving out of the location to break out from your ex-lover. If you're dedicated to saving your relationship, you'll want to do what it takes. There are constantly special jobs and unique houses. You'll in no way have every different marriage much like the only you have got were given have been given.

MAKING AMENDS VS. APOLOGIZING

We say "I'm sorry" so frequently that the phrases frequently lose their which means. It seems like an easy 'get out of jail free' card to toss out at the equal time as you've finished a few thing wrong, and magically the whole lot's adequate.

When it includes infidelity, announcing "I'm sorry" are in no way going to be enough to undo the harm because of your cheating. Not simplest that, however it could additionally sound insulting inclusive of you're disregarding the enormity of what happened.

Making amends takes things to the subsequent level. It is the way of understanding the quantity of what you've done and finding a one-of-a-kind manner. It is a life-style choice in preference to a one-off gesture. It is a few issue that calls for repeated movement, area, and a focal point on the prolonged-term destiny of your relationship. Moreover, it places the focal point in your companion in place of yourself. You are accomplishing out to them to reveal you still care and want to position their desires as your most priority.

HOW DO I KNOW MY PARTNER IS READY TO MAKE AMENDS?

As we've already discussed, phrases aren't sufficient in terms of rebuilding your relationship. If you're the individual that's been betrayed, you'll be so used to listening to lies that it's no wonder you're suffering with believing your associate at the same time as they're saying they need to location subjects right.

There are some matters a very good way to will let you recognize your partner is ready to make amends:

They are empathic closer to you. They make an lively try to pay interest for your needs and meet them with their actions.

They can disagree with you in healthful and powerful techniques. It's natural so you could have arguments on the road to restoration. It's the manner you cope with the ones disagreements that indicates you whether or now not or not your partner is certainly willing to make amends. If your accomplice is capable of take your view on board with out casting aspersions on you, that is a exceptional sign that they're prepared to do topics in any other case.

They use their movements to reveal they care. Talk is reasonably-priced. Now is the time to your accomplice to show you the way a good deal they need to rebuild topics. If you spot a concerted attempt to willingness to do subjects in any other way, take want from it.

They apprehend the need to earn your don't forget. It's going to take time, and they acquire that and provide you with what you want to start trusting all over again— regardless of how prolonged it takes.

I've been unfaithful – how can I make amends?

There are many advantages to developing amends:

It gives you emotional consolation in a manner not anything else can. It lets in you to recognise you've accomplished the whole lot you can to restore the damage, irrespective of the outcome.

It allows you sense exceptional approximately your self. It takes plenty of braveness to confess to what you've completed and be willing to do a little thing fantastic about it. You need to understand that that is a massive deal and deliver yourself credit score score score for that.

It can help restore get hold of as true with. Actively demonstrating you're running in your dating offers your accomplice a smooth sign that you're well worth trusting once more.

It allows you to remedy unfinished conditions. You've placed an surrender to your affair, and now you're equipped to move in advance collectively in conjunction with your companion.

It reduces worry and stress. Everything's out inside the open, and also you don't need to worry your partner finding out your secrets and strategies because they comprehend them all.

Still, it is able to be difficult to recognize in which to begin. One approach I like to apply with my clients is the H.U.R.T. Method:

H – Hurt

Tell your partner what you possibly did to harm them. Don't get into the motives why or what your motives had been. Simply percentage the statistics of the situation.

U – Understanding

Tell your companion how you watched your behavior made them enjoy and famend and validate them.

R – Remorse

Express regret for what you probable did and tell your partner the manner it makes you enjoy approximately yourself. This goes deeper than pronouncing sorry—dive into why you're sorry and what exactly you remorse approximately your moves.

T – Time

Let your associate understand it's going to take time to heal your relationship, and you're willing to give it as prolonged because it takes. By the same token, it's going to take time to cope with your very very own troubles so you don't stray another time, and also you'd like your partner to permit you that time so that you can each build a destiny collectively.

EMOTIONAL RESTITUTION (FOR THE ONE WHO WAS UNFAITHFUL)

Earlier on this e-book, we looked at Full Disclosure, wherein the accomplice who cheated took ownership of what happened with a focus on their betrayal. Accepting obligation for what you've finished modified into truely the first step in making amends. Now you're going to build on that with emotional restitution, which places the spotlight on how your infidelity has harm the ones around you, mainly your associate.

Start through manner of creating an emotional restitution declaration. This encapsulates what you're willing to do on an ongoing basis to make amends and heal your dating.

Your announcement can also appearance a few element like this:

I am devoted to shifting ahead with my husband/spouse, acknowledging that we've each been harm via my moves. I take transport of the outcomes of my infidelity and will paintings on processing my grief over what took place while assisting my husband/spouse to paintings through theirs. I am willing to discover the facts of my infidelity and the surrounding emotions with my husband/partner. I am devoted to strolling together with my husband/spouse to overcome the diverse problems my infidelity has added about us.

Let's harm this down a bit in addition:

I am dedicated to moving ahead with my husband/spouse, acknowledging that we have each been damage through using my actions.

While you had been having an affair, you were being deceitful and leaving behind your marriage. With this assertion, you're locating out to live in the fact of your relationship, although it's painful. And wherein the pair of you revel in harm and suffering, you're agreeing to stand this pain head-on in preference to looking for to keep away from it. You are walking collectively on this in choice to continuing to desolate tract your marriage.

I gather the results of my infidelity and will artwork on processing my grief over what befell whilst assisting my husband/partner to artwork thru theirs.

Your moves have fee each of you dearly. You've out of place the wedding you belief you had. As we've already noted, you need to grieve this. While you could do this through yourself, while you pick out to art work through your grief collectively, you open yourself as a good buy as a restoration technique that would bring you each collectively, so neither of you has to feel on my own.

I am inclined to discover the records of my infidelity and the encompassing feelings with my husband/spouse.

Difficult despite the fact that it can be, you want to technique what came about, so it doesn't occur again. This is going to be hard, and it's herbal to want to avoid doing this, but in case you're crucial approximately being straightforward any further, it's an essential a part of the restoration journey. You want to be open to discussing your affair as an lousy lot as critical, which can be loads while you first begin walking via it. Be open to exploring each you and your companion's feelings and stories. This is the way you're going to technique and assimilate it to transport past it.

I am devoted to strolling collectively with my husband/wife to conquer the diverse problems my infidelity has delivered about us.

Your affair has made life tough for both of you. That's a truth you'll want to address. If you're capable of work thru it collectively, you'll every emerge as in a miles better vicinity down the road.

Chapter 5: The Primary Question

How to Cheat Respectfully When You Are Married

Apparently Shaquille O'Neal as quickly as wrote a memoir known as "Shaq: Uncut: My Story" and he basically copped to having cheated on his ex-spouse Shaunie O'Neal - time and again. But he claimed that he didn't "do it disrespectfully." So it have been given me to thinking about this as a likely weblog post: How to Cheat Respectfully.

Now, in advance than I even start with my list, I want to mention that I don't for my part think there's a manner to cheat "respectfully." I think dishonest is basically disrespectful. And the older I get, the extra sturdy this opinion turns into. There isn't always any manner to "cheat respectfully" in a wedding, or perhaps a dating without the gain of marriage that is devoted. I recall that marriage is sacrosanct and if someone chooses to cheat even as married, my for my part view is that during all contexts it is essentially disrespectful to his or her partner.

1. Don't cheat on your partner with pals of your companion.

2. Don't bring your trollops into the marital domestic and in no way do they area their asses at the marital bed; and whilst you're at it, don't carry your trollops everywhere you've been on the facet of your spouse or in which your spouse is probably to move — like consuming places, social clubs, and such things as that. Take the trollops someplace an extended manner away!

three. Don't introduce your spouse in your lover and act as though it's not your lover and make an ass of your spouse in this way by way of manner of giving the sweetheart the pinnacle hand — which efficiently is what you do on the equal time as you are making this introduction information you're bonking the opposite man or woman, but at the same time as your accomplice is certainly oblivious to what is taking location; however even in case your companion is privy to what's taking area, don't do this. It is unseemly.

4. Don't be considering your lover at the equal time as you're making love to your spouse.

five. Don't introduce your lover to your youngsters with your partner.

6. Don't deliver your lover extra costly items than you offer your partner after which go away the receipts putting round in order that your partner will "by way of way of accident" find out them.

7. Don't use the "L" word collectively along with your lover.

8. Don't spread the affair across the circles wherein your partner travels in order that the funny story is in your spouse and each

person is in at the comic tale except your partner.

9. If you fall for the lover don't begin to treat your companion like rubbish just so they will haven't any one among a kind preference however to invite for a divorce; be a person approximately it and ask for a divorce with out resorting to treating your accomplice like garbage.

10. Never make the "mistake" of calling your spouse with the aid of manner of your lover's call.

So that turn out to be Ms. Cavendish with reference to "cheating respectfully." Did you agree or disagree along aspect her?

I agree. Makes top notch revel in

I disagree in reality

I take into account how she feels about it in my opinion however disagree collectively along with her listing

This put up is outrageous

So the following article is prepared the person of infidelity. The creator posits that infidelity is "natural" and that it's miles "unrealistic" and in all likelihood even "unfair," to keep one's companion to such an unrealistic famous. What do I anticipate? Hme…I don't think that I agree that infidelity is "herbal." I do agree that it is quite viable to look different people to whom one can also moreover sense an appeal – despite the fact that one is devoted by using manner of marriage to a person else. However, the notion that it is natural to cheat? I am not certain I am willing to make that leap. I suppose the writer makes a evaluation to unique species of animals which are polygamous. But I see a fundamental difference among human and unique species in that we were given the electricity of preference.

Ultimately, I suppose what is "herbal" is "preference" now not infidelity. One can choose out to brush aside the urge to do pills, binge drink and shoot humans within the center of Fifth Avenue in Manhattan. These subjects may additionally seem perfectly herbal to do – depending at the instances. But must one constantly do any of these gadgets below any situation? I don't assume so. One has the choice. Likewise, I do not forget that during relation to infidelity, one has a preference. It is not a query of it being natural.

It is natural and human to preference a couple of person in any given lifetime. You simplest should have a take a look at maximum other species in the animal u . S . A . To be satisfied of this. For example, dogs, cats and fowl to call satisfactory three. They are polygamous.

Monogamy is not awesome dull it is certainly unrealistic and unnatural and getting divorced due to the reality your companion "cheated" with a person else is ridiculous and passé.

Human species like particular animal species are social creatures. They have eyes and that they have got 5 senses which connects them and maintains them associated with others round them in their line of imaginative and prescient and in their environment. Attraction is as natural as eyesight. There is nothing incorrect with being interested in more than one man or woman at any given time even if you are married. The problem is the marriage settlement which is not any insignificant aspect. Infidelity is a breach of that settlement, that is actual. But one have to argue that the agreement itself is unenforceable on this element because infidelity is herbal. So this time period within the agreement is void ab initio. Being monogamous simply isn't what turn out to be supposed for the human species to be.

So that emerge as Ms. Goldstein at the individual of infidelity. Do you agree or disagree together with her?

I agree. Cheating is sincerely herbal.

I disagree. There is not anything natural approximately dishonest on your companion.

I neither agree nor disagree.

This publish is outrageous

This submit is silly and outrageous

Chapter 6: The Problem Of Faux Accusations Of Infidelity

These look like not unusual and probable one should argue that despite the fact that those allegations may want to have a terrible effect on a person's recognition, that women undergo greater reputational damage – and also are more likely to be the item of home violence – while accusations of infidelity are levelled with the useful resource of 1 partner inside the route of the other.

If, for instance, Hillary Clinton had had 3 husbands and had been accused of cheating on Bill Clinton with the sort of guys – whether or now not those accusations became out to be reality or fiction - it is questionable whether she would possibly have prolonged long gone at once to become the number one lady nominee for president of america.

From my thoughts-set, it'd appear that a person who knowingly makes the ones forms of faux accusations in the direction of their companion is a person who's deeply worried, controlling and duplicitous – and maybe even reckless and dangerous. Indeed, it might appear tyrannical for a person to knowingly do this to their partner. Who does this form of component? And what's someone to do if they will be in this case?

When Amber Heard and Johnny Depp were divorcing in 2016, Depp allegedly accused Heard of having done an affair with Billy Bob Thornton - Angelina Jolie Pitt's ex-husband.

Both Ms. Heard and Mr. Thornton reportedly vehemently denied the accusation. But that apparently did no longer stop Mr. Depp from allegedly going so ballistic at the notion, that he's rumored to have severed considered one in every of his palms and smeared blood on a wall or some such floor, in the course of his resulting meltdown.

The Depp Heard story in the end stimulated me to write this publish: How to cope with false accusations of infidelity. A short run around the Internet famous that it is a quite common hassle. A lot of other halves in severa on line discussion board can be heard discussing this trouble with their on-line friends. In this form of fora, one woman opined that her husband became projecting his personal infidelity onto her along together together with his relentless and ridiculous accusations. The hassle is that as ridiculous as the ones accusations may be now and again, they frequently result in home violence for the spouse. What can someone do?

Do no longer cheat in your companion.

Second, deny the accusations no more than three instances. If after denying three instances (and actually being innocent) your spouse maintains to accuse you, then those accusations are likely now not about you. And there may be no longer anything you can say to trade your partner's mind so that you might also additionally as properly don't say a few factor further at the trouble. Refuse to have interaction.

Third, propose marriage counseling and if your companion received't maintain in thoughts counseling and purchased't prevent with the accusations, you actually need to recall escalating the results likely in a divorce felony professional's workplace.

Fourth, make certain you could account for your time and be apparent at the side of your accomplice about in that you're and wherein you will be just so there can be tons much less thinking and speculating and suspecting taking place in this man or woman's head.

Fifth, if these accusations are being made in a public dialogue board (for instance, you are a public parent) recollect hiring a PR business enterprise to disclaim the costs and clean your nicely name.

If the man or woman you're being accused of having an affair with is privy to your accomplice, bear in mind having this character speak together along with your partner approximately the problem.

Finally, in case your spouse keeps to hassle you with out motive over a few detail as intense and as sensitive as infidelity, my can also moreover need to get the hell out of the marriage because of the reality this character have to clearly kill you at some point in a jealous rage.

Is a person who makes those kinds of allegations risky and capable of murdering their partner in a jealous rage?

Yes

I disagree. That is an excessive stop to acquire

Yes and no. People lie in a situation like this because of the truth they will be indignant.

But wherein there can be smoke there may be fireside.

This placed up is ridiculous

These conclusions are outrageous.

The next placed up deals with the notion of "guilt unfastened" infidelity. This one is a bit...sensitive...I suggest, what can I say approximately it with out sounding like I am condoning this form of element? I want to say in the most effective phrases that I don't inspire or condone infidelity. But I do apprehend that subjects manifest. I think the writer of the positioned up is also of that college of idea that, topics seem, human beings are adults, they make their personal selections, and inside the occasion that they pick out to cheat, proper proper right here are a few methods to make it plenty much less...lousy. What can I say or upload to that? Nothing.

eleven WAYS TO HAVE A GUILT FREE AFFAIR

1. Get under the influence of alcohol whenever you do it.

2. Build up a wholesome contempt on your accomplice at the ideal moments to justify your terrible acts.

three. Write down the reasons for your terrible acts so that you can see virtually why it's no huge deal which you are breaking your dedication to be truthful until dying do you element. Do pros and cons in a chart in order that you will be actual smooth on why that is right.

four. Take care of factors at home first, so that everyone is happy. (Wink, wink)

5. Be up the the front and honest that you're having an affair (at least he or she will't call you a "mendacity" cheat on pinnacle of being a cheat – be sincere approximately your dishonest!)

6. Be easy on your intentions just so there aren't any impolite surprises. All affected

activities need to realise your actual intentions. If you'll by no means are trying to find a divorce out of your associate and are handiest having a outstanding time, make that clean to anybody concerned. It's better.

7. Use prophylactics, normally, so it's no longer like you will be bringing home greater marital heirs lest your bowled over partner takes greater-judicial measures to rectify the situation.

8. Regularly go to confession after each episode of infidelity to wipe the slate clean.

9. Do it high-quality for research on a ebook, in which case, it doesn't in reality depend.

10. Do it with someone who's furthermore married or in a devoted dating. Can you virtually name this adultery if both people are thankfully married to unique humans?

11. Don't divorce your accomplice for the paramour – not even in case you fall in love with the paramour.

So what do you located? Did this publish ruffle your feathers or tickle your fancy? Do you accept as true with Jeannie or do you disagree?

I agree, as an alternative

I agree absolutely

I strongly disagree, she's out of her thoughts. Cheating can never be "guilt-free"

This is so stupid!

Chapter 7: Infidelity Does Not Constantly Result In Divorce

But it once in a while sooner or later finally ends up developing new heirs to the circle of relatives coffers. Sometimes, that's right, toddlers mysteriously get conceived. Is this a deal breaker for maximum humans? I want to think so. I could possibly furthermore bear in mind that most customarily than now not, at the same time as new lifestyles is created due to infidelity that the marriage ultimately will implode. I truly don't recognize the stats on this. But it is my stoop. Let's pay interest what the following located up says about the hassle:

Apparently, Maria Shriver went to Christmas Eve mass together along with her brief to be ex husband Arnold Swarzenegger (wrong spelling?) and the rumor generators are on foot rampant that a reconciliation can be in the gambling playing cards. It's no longer now not viable. Women like Maria are used to their husband's incapacity to preserve the circle of relatives jewels neatly tucked away inner his flawlessly dry wiped clean pants. Let's actually face it. It's tough for lots of fellows to hold it in their dry wiped clean pants, pinnacle enough? And if every female become going to expire and cut up? There likely wouldn't be any married heterosexual couples – or gay ones for that depend - in California. But the rub is even as he is so sincerely negligent, that he sows his seed in a single-of-a-kind girls's couchies and has children with the ones humans - isn't it? Wouldn't that just rub you the incorrect manner as a girl? It's awful enough to be cheated on through your accomplice. Fine. We will bite our tongues and grit and go through it. But then this character doesn't employ prophylactics? When this man or woman impregnates this chook? When this individual brings domestic extra-marital bastards into the residence? For chrissakes. It is an excessive amount of for the common female to deal with. But reputedly, now not Maria Shriver. She appears to be rethinking her divorce filing which came about circa May 2011 and he or she or he reputedly has been "telling buddies" that her spiritual religion and other worries (aka, Arnold is such an fantastic lover I clearly don't see how I can replace him) are making her have second thoughts about the divorce — the 13 3 hundred and sixty 5 days antique more-marital son be damned....Is the phrase bastard pejorative? I feel horrible for the use of it. I can't don't forget it's however properly enough to apply this phrase, however it honestly appears to in form in a slightly outrageous kind of way. Nothing else will pretty do. I want to dam it out and use some other word. I recognize. But...allow me check the dictionary. If it's though in the dictionary! So I am leaving it...it's despite the fact that in the dictionary....Hm...it surely manner an "illegitimate" child. Hm...I don't recognise. Should I go away it in? Or take it out....I guess I will go away it in, besides a reader has robust objections to the term. Seriously if honestly all and sundry gadgets to it, I will strike it out. I don't comprehend if I even think that phrase want to be within the dictionary. Is it right to consult an innocent baby as "illegitimate?" As a "bastard?" Shouldn't all children be taken into consideration as "valid" virtually via way of particular characteristic of their start, of their sovereign proper as a man or women to exist? WT_ is that, relating to kids as "bastards?" and as "illegitimate?" And having that in the dictionary in 2011-2012? This bothers me. I experience like I want to not use that phrase to consult kids. It seems incorrect...but perhaps I'm being hypersensitive, as not unusual...it's virtually that it takes area to me that each man or women is legitimate as long as she or he is born. No depend what the situations. That is what I think is correct and suitable...

Anyway, my hat is off to Maria. And women like her. That isn't an smooth state of affairs to circumnavigate and to forgive. And to think it changed into her maid, for chrissakes! What is that? That is a weird shape of speech at the same time as your husband leaves your bed and is going to bonk the maid. Seriously. What is that saying to a spouse at the same time as a husband does that? And then has children??? And Maria forgives that??? I don't recognize. I'm a completely forgiving person. But I don't understand if I may want to forgive that, in my opinion. So I sincerely apprehend ladies like Maria who've the belly to appearance past a few factor like that.

So, what do you suspect? Putting aside the "bastard" question and the "French" used by Goldstein, can also moreover need in your marriage stay in this degree of betrayal? Obviously, Maria Shriver and Arnold Schwarzenegger's marriage did now not live to tell the tale. It is doubtful whether it became the existence of the child, or simply the infidelity itself that prompted the dying of that marriage but the marriage has prolonged given that imploded. Could your marriage live on a scenario like Maria's or it is unforgivable and consequently a deal-breaker for you as nicely?

The creator & Maria are proper. This is too much to forgive and is a deal-breaker, actually.

I can't get past the writer's use of the phrase "bastard" this is wildly beside the point. How may additionally need to you print that?

I disagree. It's no large deal if children are the end stop end result of infidelity. Things seem. It's truly forgivable.

It's simplest unforgivable if it's the spouse that receives pregnant. If it's far the individual that knocks up someone, what's the large deal?

The subsequent submit offers with this problem of being blind-sided by way of using using other people's infidelity even as you are not even within the marriage your self. Has that ever came about to you? Where a person else pronounces their divorce because of infidelity and you're so shocked, so blind-sided, so affronted, that it is nearly as although it is you? For example, in the highlighted placed up from Divorce Saloon under, once I study Jeannie's preliminary response to the Shriver/Schwarzenegger divorce, it honestly resonated and I have become nodding my head as I become studying due to the truth I think this is exactly how I reacted within the beginning as quickly as I heard that that precise couple changed into divorcing due to a scandal like that. My shock changed into visceral. And then I began to impeach myself. Why did it depend to me so much? Why did I care sufficient to render an opinion in this marriage among those human beings even as they'll be widespread strangers to me? Obviously I don't understand either of these human beings and best see them on television. So I don't understand why I felt that via hook or with the aid of criminal this gave me insights into their marriage – as even though thru some technique I had a private right to apprehend what come to be taking place, what had passed off and why it had happened. It begged the questions: Why are we able to fixate on special people's relationships and marriages and divorces to the amount that we do to the detail that one birthday celebration's infidelity in that marriage renders us moot with surprise? And secondly, while a public determine commits an act or acts of infidelity, is the wrongdoing via hook or by using criminal greater in price than if the act modified into devoted through an unknown character in society?

WHEN INFIDELITY SHOCKS

Maria Shriver and Arnold Schwarzenegger Split! OMG. Well, I actually have turn out to be settling myself at the sofa this morning, with my cup of ginger tea (love ginger tea!) to have a look at The View - a display I certainly have now not seen in how prolonged? - and I heard Barbara Walters say some aspect preposterous approximately the Shriver/Schwarzenegger 25 yr marriage and mentioned how difficult it is to preserve a wedding.

Happier Days for Schwarzenegger & Shriver

So I actually have emerge as to the character sitting throughout from me and gasped:

"The Schwarzeneggers have grow to be divorced???" And she nodded, "tremendous, didn't you pay attention?"

And I become like, "no, of course I didn't listen. When did this take area???"

And she said she'd heard it in advance on Good Morning America.

And I in truth idea, "Wow. I surrender. There's not anything sacred anymore. There isn't any marriage this is certainly worth bragging approximately. All marriages are at risk of divorce and infidelity..."

Wow. Arnold and Maria are getting a divorce. Imagine that. That is even more unexpected than even as Al and Tipper Gore brought their split. I mean, you honestly study high quality humans and you believe you studied they have this solid, impenetrable marriage, you recognize? You purchase into this fallacy and this fable that they may be satisfied and that they may be this exemplary situation and this couple to be modern day or maybe envied in a few techniques. Because they have been given it. They have the correct marriage.

And then you definately in reality study that Schwarzenegger had a predilection for "groping" distinct women and that he had a infant out of wedlock you pass, "whaaaat????" And you wonder how masses this factored into the marriage. Or the demise of it.

Wow. I'm actually greatly surprised, I clearly have to say. They appeared like one of these storybook couple: The massive he-man with the bulging muscle tissues, and the comely Kennedy princess with the entire head of hair who moved to the Pacific Coast and had 3 cute children....

Wow. Well, at least this appears to be an amicable state of affairs. They are fine separated at this factor. They haven't but filed for divorce, even though I am certain that is a precursor. I don't assume this to get nasty, although. I is probably really surprised, possibly even disappointed, if that takes area.

Jeeze. Well, what can I say? The greater I bear in mind it, the greater I assume I am not missing out on a few element with the useful useful resource of in no manner having gotten married. Because I don't need a divorce after I get married. I need the storybook completing, or I don't need the wedding. I want truely one husband, to broaden antique with, or I don't want any. And based completely totally on what I see, I think possibly that isn't very probable. Divorce is just inevitable in the end. Even for the great of them. And so, why do human beings even trouble? That is what I would love to recognize. Why do humans hassle?

Chapter 8: Choosing To Stay After Infidelity

Hillary Clinton is at the cusp of being the number one girl president of the us however first she has to get past Donald Trump who has made no bones of the fact that he plans to combat an epic, grimy, merciless conflict toward the previous First Lady. His crucial technique goes to be calling her each derogatory name inside the book and then to linking her to every debauched adulterous deed her husband, former president Bill Clinton, ever committed (or is said to have dedicated). With the latter, there is lots of fabric with which Mr. Trump can artwork. These stories has been documented only too well via an unrelenting press.

If you're vintage sufficient to have lived via the Monica Lewinsky scandal, you may keep in thoughts how devastated Hillary appeared to be via everything, how visibly humiliated with the beneficial resource of her husband's infidelity she seemed. But but she stayed. She did now not divorce him.

Most human beings as ladies applauded her for staying with him, specially as it have become around the time of his impeachment in which a divorce submitting should virtually have ended his political profession in utter shame. In brief, had Hillary Clinton dumped Bill Clinton for his infidelity, the Republicans should have without a doubt removed him from place of business - because the momentum could possibly have without a doubt blown up all spherical him and would were too hard to overcome and it would were over for Mr. Clinton's political profession.

Hillary reputation thru him, keeping his hand like that, saved his arse – and each person is aware of it. But now, Trump is accusing Hillary of being an ""enabler." He says that Bill Clinton is the largest abuser of girls and that Hillary end up an "enabler."

What do you remember this? Was she an "enabler" for staying? Should she have divorced him? If no longer, what should she have completed to shop herself this characterization as an "enabler" twenty years later? And moreover, do you suspect her probabilities of winning the presidency could were more nowadays had she left her philandering husband to the choice and mercy of Ken Starr and the GOP? Would she have greater credibility as a leader and presidential candidate? Especially with girls? Because what message did she deliver by using the usage of refusing to surrender this marriage whilst her husband so violated her receive as genuine with and their bridal ceremony vows with such beautiful acts of infidelity and betrayal?

So this is one very excessive profile instance of the partner who chooses to stay with the cheating husband. What do you consider this? Would you've got were given stayed beneath the identical set of situations?

Never

Maybe, it's miles predicated upon on what I emerge as getting out of it

Yes, if I loved my husband

Yes however I can also have him castrated to make sure this in no manner took place yet again. No, I'm very excessive!

Research suggests that for a marriage to continue to exist, and truly for infidelity fees to stay low in that unique marriage, it's miles higher if the husband earns extra money than the spouse. It seems that after women's earning strength out-strips their husbands, every spouses have a better probability of committing adultery. Indeed, it seems as despite the fact that whilst a lady makes extra money than her husband she loses recognize for him on a incredible degree. Obviously there can be exceptions to this. But via and large, it appears to appear. On the husband's problem, even as his accomplice makes extra than he does, he probably can enjoy emasculated. And this seems to persuade him to dedicate adultery, ostensibly to reveal that he is though the person and that he's despite the fact that macho no matter being out-earned thru his wife.

WHEN THE WIFE EARNS MORE THAN HER HUSBAND INFIDELITY RATES RISE ON BOTH SIDES

A cutting-edge have a observe located out that every women and men seem to love it better whilst the man is the precept breadwinner inside the family

Infidelity and via extension divorce expenses seem to be decided, as a minimum partially, by means of way of who "wears the pants" in the own family. If it's far the spouse, there might be problem constant with a examine completed via Cornell University.

It doesn't sincerely take a rocket scientist to determine out what the current-day day facts critiques are revealing. And that is, even as a lady has a house-husband, and while she makes extra cash than her husband, the connection quick turns into imbalanced and gender roles get all screwed up. But Cornell University researchers these days got here out with a have a look at that legitimizes the apparent: if a woman makes more than her husband, if a lady is the precept bread winner inside the own family, if a woman has a house husband, her marriage is in greater jeopardy of finishing in divorce than if the inverse turn out to be real.

The check simply confirmed that divorce fees are higher for guys who make a whole lot much less than their better halves. First of all, men whose better halves make extra money than they do had been more likely to cheat on their wives. As the Daily Mail located it, it's likely due to the fact they're able to't face up to all the "yummy mommies at the playground." But the ones guys moreover exhibit a experience of powerlessness and "gender identification danger" at the same time as their wives out-earn them. And really in order that they cheat to reaffirm that they wear the pants inside the circle of relatives, ordinary with the take a look at.

Also, even as a lady's income a ways outpaces her husband's she is likewise more likely to cheat on him, and to be disappointed with him as a husband, steady with the studies completed within the have a observe.

All of this improved the possibilities of divorce for that couple and so the rate of divorce is surely higher for couples on this control institution.

The opposite is not authentic, but. When someone out-earns a spouse, the wedding is heaps plenty much less probable to result in divorce and he or she or he's less in all likelihood to cheat on him. It additionally can be inferred from the Cornell examine that if the events make sort of the equal profits, the issues of infidelity, dissatisfaction and dishonest although exists. Something within the male DNA (and in all likelihood the lady too), dreams for the character to make extra cash and to be the primary breadwinner for the man or woman to feel powerful, in control, and, frankly, to feel greater like someone. When someone appears like a person in his relationship, he's much less probable to cheat; and he has partner who is happier and moreover plenty less in all likelihood to cheat. And feeling like a person appears at once related to how plenty cash he brings home. We can mess with nature all we want. Some fundamental subjects are in no way going to change.

But that's no longer often a data-flash. I figured that out as soon as I turned into approximately ten years vintage. Don't realize why it took a test at Cornell for the press to be throughout the apparent.

So what do you observed? Is the look at bogus? Or is there some component to this phenomenon? Why may a spouse's larger paycheck lead her husband to cheat on her.

I think this observe is bogus. Seriously.

It makes entire revel in. Everybody is aware of that guys like to enjoy just like the agency and having a accomplice with extra money will emasculate him.

This is sincerely nonsense.

I make greater than my husband and it's far running just incredible

My spouse makes extra and it does now not trouble me the least bit. I may want to now not cheat due to that.

Chapter 9: Is Face Book A Portal To Infidelity?

New York Magazine once wrote that "divorce legal professionals want to thank Mark Zuckerberg for his portal to infidelity" Much ado has been made about the mal impact that Facebook is having on the united states of america's marriages. For some uncommon cause, cheating spouses seem to have an affinity for the social media network and use it to perpetrate their adulterous trysts. Even the American Academy of Matrimonial criminal professionals has weighed in with records of what number of divorce prison professionals are the usage of Facebook to win divorce instances — a especially bewildering situation, due to the fact the entire united states of america is not any fault and there's no want anymore to expose dishonest in ANY jurisdiction on this u . S . A .. Nevertheless, proper right right here's NYM at the

Facebook/divorce dichotomy:

"Facebook's toll at the agency of marriage isn't always any wonder to Cedric Miller of the Living World Christian Fellowship Church, who called it a 'portal to infidelity' for allowing clients to reconnect with former enthusiasts. There's quite a few emphasis on exes. But what approximately the get entry to social networks can offer to capacity new enthusiasts? Features like 'People You Might Want to Cheat With Later If Things Aren't Going So Well' represents a doubtlessly untapped marketplace. For Facebook, we suggest."

So, are you saying that Facebook in truth has a characteristic called "people you would in all likelihood need to cheat with later if topics aren't going so nicely?" is that for real? Or is the author of the piece simply giving them thoughts? Well, regardless of the case may be, it appears well settled that Facebook is horrific news for cheaters who want to stay married. Frankly, why does all and sundry get on Facebook? I am having problem getting why parents insist on setting their dirty laundry up on Facebook. Are you on Facebook? Am I the best individual not on Facebook?

So are you on Facebook? Do you accept as true with you studied it encourages infidelity? Would you furthermore mght describe Facebook as a portal to infidelity?

Yes, Facebook is the devil for marriages and it have to be banned

Yes and No. Facebook can inspire infidelity but it's far as much as the character if they will cheat or not.

No. Infidelity starts offevolved in someone's very personal thoughts and it's their very very own evil. Don't blame Facebook.

I don't recognize some thing approximately Facebook. I am no longer on it. Next question please.

Cheating with an ex does seem a bit particular, doesn't it? Let's flow into right now to Goldstein on this one:

CHEATING WITH YOUR EX EVEN THOUGH YOU ARE BOTH RE-MARRIED

They divorced. They married wonderful human beings. Now they may be dishonest on their spouses – with every exclusive! I certainly have been given this one from a Dear Abby column. I concept, "Rich. Really wealthy. Why get divorced and re-married in case you are going to try this? What is incorrect with the two of you?"

I guess some people simply want the brink they get from cheating to get going. It is like a drug, a vice. Isn't it weird how dishonest can genuinely excite some people, and with different humans, it clearly dries them up. It's absolutely bizarre & thrilling.

But I find out this case barely disturbing, to be frank, this perception of cheating together together along with your ex for your associate. This is traumatic. I propose, in case you although need every special, stay married. Don't marry distinctive humans after which cheat on them in the back of their backs with every unique. That is truly grimy. But in an useless, annoying way. There is not something attractive approximately it the least bit about this style of dirtiness.

What do you suspect? Do you bear in mind Goldstein in this? Is there a few issue specially debauched and evil about dishonest on a current partner with an antique partner? My view is that humans have to be forgiven inside the event that they get divorced and later discover that they'll be nonetheless in love with every exceptional. I best fault them inside the occasion that they continue to cheat on their new spouses. I don't suppose that that is both honest or appropriate.

Is it a form of....Depravity? A particular diploma of depravity to cheat to your new accomplice collectively together with your ex-accomplice?

No it isn't wicked in any respect. It is regular

Don't be so prudish. This is how it's far in recent times.

Yes it's miles simply fucking wicked and it happened to me and I am irritated about it.

Maybe it's just love?

Chapter 10: Is Cheating Contagious?

Forget approximately whether or not divorce is contagious. Now the query is, is devious contagious too? I noticed this byline on the quilt of a style magazine this morning on the equal time as I became at Walgreens shopping for toiletries. It turned into a provocative inquiry, for effective. I didn't have time to study the factor, however I concluded, right now, that dishonest probable is, clearly, contagious — just like divorce.

And why is that? Well, because of the fact monkey see, monkey do! That's why. Pure and easy. People love to do what every body else spherical them is doing.. If your partner hears that your first-rate buddy's partner is devious and having scandalicious affairs on the place of business with bodacious brunettes, bet what? In his brain (or her mind) jealousy pops in. It's like, why want to honestly anyone else have all the amusing? They want in on all of the amusing, too. This is manifestly risky for your marriage - truly as even though human beings round you have been getting divorced. That's risky to your marriage too.

The nice aspect is, every now and then when those round you are playing around at the back of their associate's lower again (and about it) it is able to additionally make you more paranoid. You want to start distrusting your very own partner and this will cause issues — even actual cheating in case you call wolf too much on the equal time as there was no wolf. So your buddies' cheating should lead you to nag your companion and the nagging ought to lead your companion to actually begin cheating on you out of frustration.

The fine solution? If you listen your friends are dishonest on every incredible, don't even speak it collectively with your spouse. Get your marriage away from that. That's my grand conclusion. Get away from it for the sake of your self and the sake of your associate and the sake of your marriage. Because it's going to best damage your marriage and you'll be divorced right away with toxicity like this floating spherical your air.

And your friends whose cheating precipitated this? They probable weathered the storm and stayed married and if now not? Misery likes corporation. They are secretly relieved that theirs is not the pleasant marriage that cracked up.

What are your thoughts in this hassle? Do you suspect that cheating is contagious?

Yes, completely.

Maybe however I am now not so positive

This is a cop out. A manner responsible your buddies for the rot to your marriage

The jury is out. Ask me approximately this as quickly as I truely have had my morning coffee.

So this question have come to be presently tackled on divorce saloon through Brenda Monteau. It poses and exciting state of affairs: Are one night time time stands more or a great deal much less adverse to marriages than long term affairs? Or are long time amorous affairs much more likely to lead to divorce? Why of these forms of infidelity is greater unfavorable to a wedding?

I am no longer certain what I anticipate the answer is to this question. Monteau seems to complete that it relies upon and I suppose in the long run, I want to agree:

ONE NIGHT STAND OR LONG TERM LOVE AFFFAIR, Which ONE WILL MORE LIKELY LEAD TO DIVORCE?

I suppose it's far a toss-up. I suppose either a one night time stand or a long term love affair can cause divorce relying on the times.

For example, a one night time stand may additionally want to just be a "meaningless fling" to the person committing the deed, but what if it has more long lasting and far-undertaking outcomes which includes the contraction of a contamination or the appearance of a toddler? It additionally is based upon on who the best night time time time stand have become with. I might keep in mind for some spouses, it doesn't endure in thoughts who it become with. The unfaithfulness and act of betrayal — regardless of the reality that it most effective passed off as quickly as – is enough to ruin accept as true with. But for others, this can be an extenuating circumstance. If it have emerge as with a entire stranger, then relying on the alternative elements within the tale, it likely could be forgivable. But if it changed into with a person alongside facet a friend or family member, co-employee or, god forbid, a rival neighbor, this may tip the scales to unforgivable and hence harm the wedding.

Where this event occurs moreover subjects. It is probably a one night time stand however did it get up in the domestic of the couple? Did it arise somewhere that has sentimental rate to the couple? This must count quantity.

When it takes area moreover subjects – even though that is simplest a one night stand. Was it in your associate's birthday or bridal ceremony anniversary for example? Was it on a night or day that held precise significance for the circle of relatives? While it turned into taking region did the family "need" you at home due to a lifestyles and loss of life emergency? This may want to tip the scales.

How it takes region moreover subjects. Did you go away a footprint and lipstick stains and emails, films, texts and voicemails that showed you had a wicked indifference to your marriage at the time of the act? This should tip the scales.

With that all being stated, I expect below ordinary instances, the long term love affair form of infidelity is extra adverse to the marriage. This is a repeat offense and suggests a degree of intimacy and willpower this is concerning, I need to think, for a associate.

So what's your take in this? Do you recall Monteau or do you disagree?

I don't have a take. I couldn't care masses a lot less.

Obviously, one night time time stands are worse than long term amorous affairs

I count on long term affairs are infinitely more negative than one night time time time stands

Monteau is proper. It is a toss up. It relies upon on the situation.

What a stupid query!

Chapter 11: Does Cheating Affect The Amount Of Alimony

Lawmakers in West Virginia want to make an hassle of infidelity. Right now in West Virginia, and in maximum, if no longer all, special states, infidelity is irrelevant in terms of asset distribution in a divorce. In other phrases, it doesn't normally depend who did what. "Fault" does not issue into whether or not or not or not you may split (besides in case you live in New York which mandates a evidence of fault earlier than a divorce can be granted). And fault did no longer generally element into whether or now not you'll get spousal help and whether or no longer or now not you need to pay spousal help, or possibly how plenty to procure or have been ordered to pay.

But if lawmakers have their way, an first-rate way to rapid alternate. West Virginia and a handful of numerous states like Arizona are pushing to make fault depend variety in a divorce – if infidelity is a trouble.

They need the regulation to view infidelity as a form of "misconduct," normal with evaluations. Those who oppose the diploma accept as true with that those bills will simplest boom the extensive variety of combative divorces and possibly inspire extra violence in amongst spouses. And they do have aspect. But it isn't always truely ridiculous to signify that the cheater want to go through the higher culpability in a divorce, and that, particularly in no fault states, there need to be a few results to their movements – MONEY – that would make the wronged partner experience just a little little bit of vindication.

What do you bear in mind this? I did a bit little little bit of surfing and it seems that states like West Virginia do in reality offer courts authority to do not forget adultery in alimony awards. This may want to artwork in each tips: if the cheater has the manner to pay, they may be ordered to pay greater based totally mostly on the infidelity. If the opportunity partner is the financially disadvantaged accomplice but is the spouse that cheated, the alimony may be denied!

What is your take in this alimony query? Should infidelity have an effect on the quantity of alimony a person gets?

Absophockinglutely!

Infidelity is a ethical trouble. Alimony is purely economic. Apples and oranges ought to now not aggregate.

No. I don't trust in punishing people for his or her bodily desires

If the regulation permits the court docket to keep in thoughts it, then the court docket docket docket must consider it in making the award.

What the hell do I care?

Few guys appear to regret cheating on their better halves notwithstanding the truth that the infidelity consequences inside the destruction in their marriage – consistent with a have a test that changed into finished in recent times. Why is that? Is it that husbands blame their better halves for their (the husbands') transgressions outside of the wedding? Is it the spouse's fault at the same time as the husband cheats?

DO CHEATING SPOUSES REGRET THEIR CHEATING WAYS IF THE MARRIAGE ENDS IN DIVORCE?

Men's Health Magazine on divorce & cheating: A modern-day study well-knownshows that seventy seven% of married cheaters "don't have any regrets." The New York Post opinions that a Men's Health Magazine have a study famous that a whopping seventy seven% of men who cheat on their better halves haven't any regrets if the dishonest ends in divorce and eighty one% of those guys surveyed additionally stated they had been happier with their new sex lives, submit-matrimony.

www.ingramcontent.com/pod-product-compliance
Lightning Source LLC
Chambersburg PA
CBHW050004070726
47592CB00018B/709